HIS OWN El

Other Books by Keith Booth

Atherton's Progress: From Kensington Oval to Kennington Oval

Knowing the Score: The Past, Present and Future of Cricket Scoring

HIS OWN ENEMY

The Rise and Fall of Edward Pooley

Keith Booth

Foreword by Wayne James

The best wicket-keeper in the world   C W Alcock 1872

His own enemy   *Wisden* Obituary 1908

BELMONT BOOKS

First published in Great Britain in 2000 by

BELMONT BOOKS

6 Kingswood Drive

Sutton Surrey SM2 5NB

ISBN 0 9537766 0 3

A catalogue record for this book is available from the British Library

Printed by Esparto Digital Ltd, Slack Lane, Derby DE22 3DS

Cover design by Alex Smitheringale

To Ronald, Natalie and Michael

CONTENTS

Keith Booth is Scorer to Surrey County Cricket Club. A Yorkshireman by birth, he was educated at Guisborough Grammar School and Reading University where his graduation with an honours degree in French was followed by a career in retailing and university administration which took him to Nottingham, Bradford, Dundee, Johannesburg, Durham and London. In 1992, he retired to pursue a second career and in between his county and international scoring commitments, including Pakistan in the 1999 World Cup, he is fast developing a reputation as an author. This is his third book (after *Atherton's Progress* and *Knowing the Score*) and his first biography. His wife, Jennifer, is Archivist of the Tate Gallery and Surrey's reserve scorer. They live in Sutton with their two cats, Polly and Herbert.

ACKNOWLEDGEMENTS

I am most grateful for the invaluable help given by the staff of the following Libraries, Archives and Museums -

Auckland Public Library, New Zealand
British Newspaper Library, Colindale
Centre for Kentish Studies
Chepstow Museum
Chepstow Public Library
Family Records Centre
Gwent County Record Office
Islington Central Reference Library
London Metropolitan Archive
Minet Library, Lambeth
Perth Museum and Art Gallery
Richmond Local Studies Library
Suffolk County Record Office
Surrey County Cricket Club Library
Surrey County Record Office

and extend my special thanks to a number of individuals who have taken time and effort to help with the research and in a number of other ways

Fred Allen, for his research into local Belfast newspapers;
Philip Bailey, for the provision of Pooley's first-class career statistics;
Jane Baxter, Local Studies Librarian at Richmond, for drawing my attention to the Pooley entry in the 1851 Census of Population;
Stephen Chalke, for some sound advice on self-publishing;
Dave Clement, Chepstow Cricket Club, for permission to use the 1838 membership list;
Brian Cowley, for statistical information on the Pooley-Southerton combination;
Yvette Flexman, for her help in researching the *New Zealand Herald and Daily Southern Cross*;
Jeff Hancock, Surrey C C C Librarian, for tolerating my snooping into the more obscure corners of his reference library;
Henry Hodges of the Chepstow Society, for his help in securing permission to use the illustration of Lower Church Street, Chepstow;
Martin Humphreys of the Ronald Grant Film Archive, for information on the Renfrew Road Workhouse;
Wayne James (who eclipsed Pooley's world wicket-keeping record after 128 years) for contributing the Foreword;
Margaret Keelan of SDG (Strategic Decisions Group) for information on the current use and ownership of 22 The Green, Richmond;
Viscount Massereene & Ferrard, for information on Pooley in Northern Ireland;

Susan Payne, Principal Officer, Human History, Perth Museum and Art Gallery, Perth and Kinross Council, for information on Pooley's time in Perth;

Robin Pearson, Secretary, Richmond Cricket Club;

Dave, Jason and Julian Pooley, for their enthusiastic, but vain attempts to establish a link with the subject;

Ronald and Natalie Pooley, the subject's grandson and great granddaughter, for their unstinting efforts to reconstruct parts of the life of one who is still regarded as the family reprobate;

Derek Scott, Hon Secretary of the Irish Cricket Union, for information on Pooley's period in Northern Ireland;

Helen Smith and all the staff of Esparto, for their efficient and prompt service;

Alex Smitheringale, for the cover design;

Michael Thwaites, great grandson of Edward Pooley, for information about the family today and his invaluable help in constructing the family tree;

Mrs Mercedes Waters, for permission to use her drawing of Lower Church Street, Chepstow;

my mother, for helping with the proof-checking and improving the punctuation of my often comma-less prose;

finally, my wife Jennifer, for the layout of the illustrations, her expertise as a professional archivist in pointing me in the right genealogical directions and her general assistance, support and tolerance throughout the whole Pooley project.

FOREWORD

by Wayne James

(Wayne James is the holder of the World Record for the number of dismissals by a wicket-keeper in a first-class match: until 1996, Edward Pooley was one of three joint holders of a record which had stood unchallenged for 128 years)

When asked by Keith to write the Foreword for his latest project, HIS OWN ENEMY, it brought home to me the events of some four years ago when, playing for Matabeleland against long time rivals Mashonaland for the Logan Cup (Zimbabwe's First-Class Competition), greatly assisted by a line-up of quality bowlers, I unknowingly broke Edward Pooley's World Record for the highest number of dismissals in a First-Class Match. For my name to appear alongside some of the truly great wicket-keepers is an honour indeed.

Having obviously never seen Edward Pooley in action but read various pieces describing his skills, I can only assume that for him to have set this record on what must surely have been the low, slow pitch conditions of England in the 1860s, he must have been a gifted and accomplished keeper. One can understand records of this nature coming out of Australia, South Africa or to a lesser extent Zimbabwe, where the wickets are traditionally faster and offer more bounce, but for the record to have been set in Surrey and for it to have stood for 128 years, is true testimony to a man once described as " Surrey's Greatest Stumper".

Wayne James
Bulawayo
Zimbabwe
January 2000

PREFACE

I first began noticing the name of Edward Pooley when researching the Surrey County Cricket Club minutes for references to scoring, scorers, scorecards and scoreboards for my last book, *Knowing the Score: the Past, Present and Future of Cricket Scoring.* It was a name which seemed to appear far more regularly than that of any other current or retired professional cricketer over the period 1866 to 1907 - usually for disciplinary reasons during his playing career, then afterwards in connection with his search for work and money.

Add to this a sentence in Surrey's 150th Anniversary brochure which described him as "erratic of temper and demeanour" and referred readers to his beguiling yet sorrowful life story when they hear some drab modern hailed as a "character". Fine, but where was this story? Certainly not in any one place, but rather spread through various one and two page contemporary appreciations, 19th century newspaper reports and reference books, a few obituaries, the odd magazine article, a few paragraphs in Surrey histories and peripheral references in several books on the life of his contemporary, W G Grace......This short book is an attempt to draw them together in one volume and try and arrive at a portrait of Pooley, the cricketer and the man.

"Biography," says Robertson Davies in *The Cornish Trilogy*, "has to rely on some evidence but a great deal of speculation." There is some speculation here on for instance the respective effects of Pooley's family background, the social environment and professional cricket milieu on what he subsequently became, but basically I have tried to rely on what limited written and anecdotal evidence exists.

Some biographical tools such as diaries, scrapbooks, family photographs, interviews with friends and family, which could have shed light on the life of a more recent subject, have not been available. Pooley died in 1907, just over a year before Sir Donald Bradman was born so, although he overlapped for a few years with people the age of Lord Denning or the Queen Mother, there is no one around now with any clear recollection of him. Attempts to trace descendants through current day Pooleys of my acquaintance (Jason of

Middlesex CCC and his father, Dave, and Julian of the Surrey County Record Office) proved fruitless. I could find no definite evidence that he married, but at least two of his sisters did, so it seemed at least probable that there were a few great-great-nephews and nieces around who might be harbouring second and third-hand recollections and maybe the odd photograph or manuscript document. Eventually, however, the Law of Diminishing Returns began to kick in and I was coming to the conclusion that extra research effort would not be justified by the results.

Then, just as I was about to go to press, two great-grandchildren of Edward Pooley, quite independently of each other, contacted the Librarian at The Oval for information about their famous - or infamous - ancestor. Serendipity rules, OK. Jeff Hancock pointed them in my direction and I was able to supply each of them with a copy of what a few days earlier I had considered to be a finished manuscript of *His Own Enemy*. In return, they were able to come up with information I was painfully aware that I lacked. Research into Censuses, Birth Certificates, Local History collections and Workhouse records had provided me with a fairly full picture of Edward's early and final years. Standard cricket reference books and newspapers had filled in the middle years as far as his career as a professional cricketer was concerned, but I had no information on his personal and family life. The absence of a marriage certificate was quickly and easily explained by the Pooley great grandchildren. Great grandfather had never got around to marrying great grandmother and grandfather was the third of eight illegitimate children fathered by Edward Pooley.

Like the soldier in the children's ballad with his musket, fife and drum, he could not marry her, for he had a wife of his own - and two legitimate daughters so, long before the sophisticated line-ups of association football and hockey, Edward had invented his own 2-4-4 system, two legitimate children, four registered in the name of his mistress and four more in his own name, ten in all, five of each. So, contrary to the firm belief of many contemporary cricketers that sex was invented in the 1960s, there was a lot of it around a hundred years earlier.

One of those children in his turn also had ten (also five of each) of whom three are still alive and it is to one of them, Ronald, his daughter, Natalie, and nephew, Michael that I am indebted for filling what had previously seemed to be an unpluggable gap. It is at once disappointing and significant that there is not a great deal of anecdotal evidence - disappointing because I would have liked to have known more, but significant because Edward Pooley, despite his illustrious cricketing career, despite his rubbing shoulders with W G Grace, was for his own family for many years a taboo subject. He was a skeleton in the family cupboard. He was not talked about. No one would blink an eyelid now; but social attitudes have changed. The stigma of illegitimacy in nineteenth century England was strong.

It is, ironically, the one extant interview with Pooley himself that has given rise to a number of errors, including crucially his date of birth and the manner of his introduction to wicket-keeping. He is one of those included in A W Pullin (Old Ebor)'s *Talks with Old English Cricketers* and while the material is invaluable for an insight into the Pooley character, factual accuracy is more honoured in the breach than the observance. Nevertheless, it has been relied on as a reputable primary source by, among others, *Wisden, The Times* and the Association of Cricket Statisticians and Historians and a number of myths and errors have filtered through into secondary sources.

It is, of course, one of the fundamental rules of serious scientific or academic research that the researcher should be reluctant to rely on a single experimental result or source, but try and find independent, corroborative evidence. It is a rule that a number of previous contributors to a Pooley canon which invites explosion have chosen to disregard and the over-reliance on Pullin has resulted in a mixture of truths, half-truths and downright untruths. A hundred years on, it is time to set the record straight.

Notwithstanding the identifying and unscrambling of those elements where Pooley has been economical with the truth, there are a couple of advantages - one historical and one geographical - in writing the biography of a nineteenth-century Londoner. Firstly, there are no copyright problems as all the material is well outside the time limit and secondly, the Family Records Centre and the London Metropolitan Archive are within spitting distance of each other and, a real bonus, within walking distance of Pooley's old Islington and Kennington haunts. The sites of Pooley residences in Newington, Battersea, Teddington and Twickenham are all easily accessible and the British Newspaper Library at Colindale is a short ride along the Northern Line. Additionally research into family records is made much easier when one is pursuing a not too common surname like Pooley and an even rarer one like that of Pooley's long term mistress, Sabine. Far more straightforward than searching for the right John Brown or Charles Smith.

Lytton Strachey took the view that the role of the biographer was to "attack his subject in unexpected places" and "shoot a sudden, revealing searchlight into obscure recesses". I would not be so presumptuous as to suggest that my biographical abilities are on the same level as Strachey's, but I hope that, having unearthed some new information, I have been able to recreate from a variety of sources the life and times of a controversial Victorian cricketer and to explore the influences which shaped his character, both on and off the field.

Keith Booth
Sutton
January 2000

CHAPTER 1

EARLY YEARS, FAMILY BACKGROUND AND RICHMOND GREEN (1842/60)

Edward Pooley was born in Richmond, Surrey, on 13 February 1838. That much is clear from those respected chronicles of the game and its players, *Wisden Cricketers' Almanack*[1] and *Who's Who of Cricketers*[2] and from that infallible source, his obituary in *The Times*.[3] Except he wasn't. He was born, Edward *William* Pooley in *Chepstow, Monmouthshire, on 13 February 1842*.

A *curriculum vitae* will change with time, as will a cricketer's career statistics, certainly during the course of a career and quite possibly afterwards as the Association of Cricket Statisticians and Historians assiduously unearths inaccuracies and corrects earlier errors. However, there are a number of entries, such as name, sex, date and place of birth which, in the great majority of cases, are fixed on Day One - or fairly close to it - and are expected to remain tolerably constant.

There is no suggestion that Edward's sex ever changed, but everything else seems to have. As far as I am aware, there has never been any reference to a second forename in any cricketing publication, nor any indication that he was born anywhere other than Richmond. There are a few entries under the name of Edward William in the *Post Office London Directory*[4] , a reference book which has no pretensions to accuracy on cricketing matters, but seems to have it right when the cricket record books do not.

Throughout his life, Pooley was known as Ted; that is well documented by his contemporaries and by himself in conversations recorded with him.

---

[1] 1998 Edition p 138
[2] 1984 Edition p 814
[3] 19 July 1907 p 10
[4] 1863 edition pp 528, 1212, 1852
   1864 edition pp 572, 1275, 1941
   1865 edition pp 576, 1288, 1970

Why, ninety-one years after his death, he should suddenly become 'Ned' in Simon Rae's recent biography[5] of W G Grace having, as far as I can see, never been called that in his life, is as mystifying as it is inaccurate.

Pooley's date of birth, however, does have a history of inconsistency. Arthur Haygarth, whose compilation of the massive *Scores and Biographies of Famous Cricketers* represents his life time's work, aimed to produce a potted biography of every cricketer who had played at Lord's, appended to the scorecard of his first appearance there. Pooley's was in 1864 and writing in 1877, Haygarth hints at a discrepancy in the date of birth. Having given it as 13 February 1843, he comments that 1842 is a possible alternative, but that he has received no definite information on the matter.[6] Like the Editors of *Playfair Cricket Annual* and *The Cricketers' Who's Who*, Haygarth was in the habit of seeking information directly from his subjects and like his successors too, he was not always completely successful.

Wisden begins recording *The Births and Deaths of Celebrated Cricketers* in 1867 [7] and until 1871 Pooley's date of birth appears as 1842 (with hindsight, the last time it was right!); then in 1872 , he suddenly becomes a year younger. His date of birth is now 1843 and remains at that for the rest of the century. Lillywhite's *Cricketers' Companion* which first appears in 1865 is consistent at 1843[8]. By contrast, the later Lillywhite's *Cricketers' Annual*, dating from 1872 and annually giving potted biographies of the country's main amateur and professional cricketers, is equally consistent in recording his date of birth as 1842. Self-evidently, one of them must be wrong. But which? Guided by the basic rules of historical evidence of enquiring who first said so and how did they know, I noted that the Editor of the "Red Lilly", the *Cricketers' Annual,* was at that time one Charles W Alcock who, among several other hats, wore that of the first paid Secretary of Surrey County Cricket Club. While human resources management was not at the same sophisticated level as it is today and the "personnel function" was not even a twinkle in the sociologist's eye, the likelihood is that there would be some form of staff records, if only for pay purposes. Alcock saw no reason to change a date of birth which appeared in the

[5] Simon Rae *W G Grace: A Life* pp 136, 545
[6] *Scores and Biographies* Vol VIII p 430
[7] p 153
[8] p 159

Annual for over a decade[9] and the balance of probabilities seems to point to 1842 rather than 1843, though there is no evidence that anyone seems to have cared very much, least of all Ted Pooley.

Coincidentally, Charles Alcock shares the same year of birth and death as Edward Pooley, but there are few other parallels. Alcock was a Northerner from Sunderland and a Harrovian, nurtured in the nineteenth century public school tradition of fortitude, self-rule and public spirit. By the time of his death in 1907, he had played a major role in establishing the FA Cup, the County Cricket Championship, professionalism and international sport. Pooley's background was different and, while in his playing days he was a world-class performer as a wicket-keeper, for well over a third of his life he seems to have been a dependent of, rather than a contributor to, society.

Early in the new century, however, the riddle of his date of birth seems to have been solved: the Lillywhite publications had ceased. *Wisden* had seen off its rival, Pooley had not been an active cricketer for almost twenty years and his date of birth had continued to appear annually in *Wisden* as 1843. Then suddenly, in 1902, he acquires another five years of life and his date of birth shoots back to 1838!

The reasons for the latter change do not take too much discovering and arise from an interview with A W Pullin (Old Ebor) towards the end of Pooley's life, which sheds light on the Pooley character, but does little for factual accuracy, in recording that while the standard chronicles of the game give the year as 1843, Pooley says that is an error for which his father was responsible, suggesting that young Ted might improve his chances of making it as a professional cricketer if he represented himself as being five years younger than he actually was.[10]

However, there are at least ten factual inaccuracies in that interview - and doubtless others less easy to check - and I had strong reservations about the accuracy of the revised date of 1838. By 1900 Pooley was an aging man in poor health with a vested interest in appearing older than he actually was and the fallibility of some of his other recollections throw this date into doubt.

---

[9] Appendix A p 137
[10] A W Pullin *Talks with Old English Cricketers* p 132

There must be practical difficulties in knocking five years off one's age in one's early twenties. It might be possible to be 53 and pretend to be 48, to be 43 and pretend to be 38, even to be 33 and pretend to be 28, but to be 23 and pretend to be 18 which he would be doing when he made his Surrey début in 1861, surrounded by his contemporaries and on the verge of becoming a public personality, stretches the imagination a little. Being 19, pretending to be 18, looks a much more feasible option.

In the same 'Old Ebor' interview, Pooley says that he left an apprenticeship in a soap merchant's office after three years in order to become a professional cricketer.[11] Faulty as his memory might have been, it is well chronicled that he made his Surrey debut in 1861. A part-apprenticeship between the ages of 15 and 18 or 16 and 19 might be convincing, one between 20 and 23 less so. In addition, Haygarth says that Pooley appeared for his native county while still very young. For "his native county", we must, of course, now read "his presumed native county" there being no record of Pooley's ever having played for Monmouthshire, but if he looked very young, 19 feigning 18 would perhaps give that impression; 23 feigning 18 would not.

Furthermore, if 1838 were correct, when he retired from first-class cricket in 1883, he would have been 45, possible but less likely than the alternatives of 40 or 41. If Pooley did fabricate his age, then it seems unlikely that he did so by five years early in his career, though he may well have made a one year adjustment. When he first presented himself at the doors of the Lambeth Workhouse in Renfrew Road in December 1898, he claimed to be 60.[12] Did he perhaps believe that the austere workhouse régime which classified its guests by sex, age, infirmity and character might be slightly less austere if he added four years to his age? It is at least a possibility: Workhouse admission, discharge and creed registers from this point are, with one exception which appears to be a clerical error[13], consistent with a date of birth of 1838 through to his death in 1907, allegedly at the age of 69, but in reality at 65.

---

[11]   Ib p 133
[12]   Renfrew Road Workhouse Religious Creed register.
[13]   On admission on 30 July 1904, his age is recorded as 68. 66 would be comsistent with other entries. He was actually 62

The sure-fire way of settling the question was to find his birth-certificate. My initial trawl was unsuccessful, always a possibility, since, although Registration of Births, Marriages and Deaths began in England and Wales in 1837, the legal responsibility for registration lay with the Registrar until 1874 when, under the Births and Deaths Registration Act of that year, it passed, in the case of a birth, to the parents.[14] The Family Records Centre houses the indexes (formerly held at Somerset House and then St Catherine's House) to almost 300 million births, marriages and deaths. Finding one of them is not too much of a problem, provided the name, date and place are known. If any details are not known, then finding the appropriate entry is still possible (though often difficult), provided the search can be narrowed to a limited range of possibilities. But there can be a number of false trails and red herrings and it costs £6.50 to acquire a certificate - which, it may turn out, pertains to someone totally different. The American girl who knew only that her ancestors were called Jones and came from Wales was going to need an infinite amount of £6.50s - and of patience!.....

I considered I had a reasonable chance of locating an Edward Pooley born in Richmond, probably in 1838 or 1843, possibly in 1842: in the interests of saving £6.50 I glossed over the entry for an Edward *William* Pooley, born in Chepstow in 1842 - but with hindsight, armed with information from the 1851 Census of Population, that was clearly the one I wanted.

The alternative was Parish Registers which cover baptisms, marriages and burials of those members of the community who were members of, or nominally members of, the Church of England, the majority of the population in fact. Those for Richmond for the period in question are housed in the Surrey County Record Office, formerly at Kingston-upon-Thames, now at Woking. There are no entries under the name of Pooley for the five years in question - not conclusive in itself, but suggesting that the family was Roman Catholic or nonconformist, that Edward was illegitimate or adopted, or perhaps that he was not born in Richmond.

When I was an undergraduate in France, one of my fellow-students was having difficulty locating his birth-certificate. On explaining this to a frustrated bureaucrat, he was met with an unsympathetic: "Comment,

---

[14] Muriel Nissel *People Count* p 28

monsieur, vous n'êtes pas né, vous?" I was still some way from reaching that conclusion, though I was beginning to understand the frustration.

Notwithstanding the absence of firm information on the date and place of birth, there is an abundance of evidence from secondary sources that much of Pooley's life was spent in Richmond. So what might the Census of Population returns tell us? Closed for a hundred years and not available to Haygarth and nineteenth century editors of *Wisden* and *Lillywhite's*, that taken on 30 March 1851 gives valuable information on the residents of no 22 The Green, a large house, probably incorporating the schoolhouse and overlooking Richmond Green itself. The building is now office accommodation, owned by the British Telecom Pension Fund and leased from them by management consultants SDG (Strategic Decisions Group). Next door but one at no 24 was - and is - *The Cricketers*, an extremely convenient hostelry for both nineteenth and twentieth century residents.

The occupants of no 22 a century and a half ago, however, were a schoolmaster, William Pooley, his wife Harriett [sic in the Census Return, but 'Harriet' elsewhere], five children, two resident scholars (schoolchildren in Victorian English, not high-powered University Readers) and a servant. The second child, aged nine and born in Chepstow was Edward Pooley.

His elder sister, Maria Elizabeth, also born in Chepstow, was thirteen at the time, two younger sisters, Irene and Eliza Jane, born in Islington were six and four and the latest arrival, Ellen, born in Richmond just six months earlier, was still in her cradle. The birth of the sixth child and second son, Frederick William, also later to play for Surrey and the United South of England XI , but with less distinction than his elder brother, was just over a year away. Although the regulations on qualification for county cricket by birth or residence were less tightly drawn than they were subsequently to become and there is no doubt about his residential qualification, it remains the case that Edward Pooley was never qualified by birth to play for Surrey.

His origins were now easily traceable, as were those of his siblings (dates and places of birth are shown in the Pooley family tree in Appendix D) and there emerged one significant fact which could not have been apparent from the 1851 Census, namely that Edward had or would have had an elder brother, Thomas William, born in 1839, who died of croup on 8 March 1842, when baby Edward was just 23 days old. And who knows the effect that might have had? The second Christian name, William, is passed on to Edward and eventually to Frederick who the new information about Thomas makes the third son and seventh and youngest child, not the second and sixth, as previously supposed.

Interestingly, Frederick's date of death is also wrong in the *Who's Who of Cricketers*, notwithstanding claims by the Editors that "for players born or dying in England and Wales, dates and places have been checked against the records of the General Register Office, London, where possible, and thus many details given will differ from previously published information".[15]   It is recorded as 14 September 1905, whereas his death certificate has 11 September 1905 - so both he and Edward seem to have slipped through the net, Edward more understandably so, being the more slippery and more elusive fish. It has no significance in itself, except that the birth and death certificates of the Pooley brothers reveal an error level of 50% in the dates and of 25% in the places of birth or death in a tome which regards itself as "the essential authority on the lives and records of all first-class cricketers to play in the British Isles" and was described by David Frith as the crown jewel in a biography bank which included the Old Ebor interviews and which, he says, must be the envy of all other sports[16]

The 1993 edition goes further, claiming on the slip-case "that practically every cricketer in the book has had those details of his life checked against a birth or death certificate." Except, it appears, Edward and Frederick Pooley. Admittedly, a sample of two from 12,000 or so is not statistically significant, but it does set one wondering how many more paste jewels there are in the crown and how much more dodgy currency there is in the bank.

Frederick's entry in the *Who's Who*, however, is still ahead of that in *Wisden*, which seems never to have been aware that he had died at all. Criteria for inclusion in the *Births and Deaths* pages have varied from time to time and have invariably been conditioned by space - or the lack of it. Until the Second World War, all known first-class cricketers are included, although, in the interests of space, those who died before 1851 are omitted from 1933 onwards and those who died before 1856 are omitted from 1936 onwards, so Edward and Frederick are both there, Edward with his date of birth wrong, Frederick with his date of death unrecorded, presumably

---

[15] Philip Bailey, Philip Thorn, Peter Wynne-Thomas *Who's Who of Cricketers* p 814
[16] *Cricket Statistician* Summer 1998 p 14

because it was not known. Post-war, further streamlining resulted in those who died before 1920 being discarded. Ergo, in 1950 Edward who played in 370 first-class matches and died in 1907 has gone; Frederick who played in four and died in 1905, as *Wisden* hasn't yet heard about it, is still there! Were he still alive, he would be a sprightly 98. By 1951, it has been assumed that Frederick is dead, rather than causing the King to be thinking about drafting a telegram for the following year, and he too has gone.

Matthew Engel's editorship of *Wisden* has resulted in some rationalisation into two lists, a *Register of Players* and *Births and Deaths*. Has-beens with over 200 first-class matches to their credit are re-instated in the latter, so Edward is back, but the Editor will now have to be invited to revert to the 1871 entry.

Edward's father, William Pooley, had married Harriet Edmonds Ferrier on 1 November 1835 in the parish of St Dunstan in Stepney.[17] Both William and Harriet were from Norwich.[18] Such Pooleys as are recorded in the Indexes to Births, Marriages and Deaths are predominantly in East Anglia, the East End of London and the West Country and William certainly seems to have associations with the first two.

He was an itinerant schoolmaster and after his marriage in Stepney, moved first to Chepstow, accompanied by his mother-in-law Elizabeth and sister-in-law, Annie[19]; then to Islington where they lived at 4 Shepperton Cottages[20], situated at the junction of what is now New North Road and Shepperton Road; then to Richmond and, tidily, two of his surviving six children are born at each place. The address on Frederick's birth certificate is Friars Lane, a narrow thoroughfare that runs from Richmond Green to the river.

The Pooleys' time in Chepstow was probably from the beginning of their married life in 1835 until about 1844. Maria was born there in 1837 and Thomas died there in 1842, so it spanned at least five years and the likelihood is that it was about nine. There is a strong clue in that there was a school situated in Lower Church Street, run by one Mrs Sarah Morgan

---

[17] International Genealogical Index and Stepney Parish Registers
[18] 1851 Census of Population
[19] 1841 Census of Population
[20] Birth certificates of Irene and Eliza Jane

from 1835 to 1844 and the probability is that it is this school with which William Pooley was associated.

Chepstow, a port and market town on the Wye, just beyond Offa's Dyke, had in 1841 a population of 3,300, a reduction of just over 200 on that of ten years earlier.[21] By 1851, however, it had increased by almost one third to 4,333.[22] Lower Church Street, the location of Mrs. Sarah Morgan's Day School - possibly at Myrtle Cottage, now part of Myrtle Place[23], adjacent to Chepstow Baptist Church, opened in 1816 - is a street of small cottages running from the town to the river and coincidentally not dissimilar from Friars Lane in Richmond. It was from the Riverside at the end of Lower Church Street that in 1840 John Frost, William Jones and Zephaniah Williams began their transportation to Tasmania (Van Diemen's Land, as it was then). They had the previous year been leaders of a Chartist insurrection designed to seize control of Newport.[24]

Some of the cottages have been used through the years for various private educational establishments, a Day School[25], an Academy or Boarding School for Gentlemen, a Middle Class School[26], a Ladies' School and at present the Riverside Nursery School.

In 1839, William Pooley joined the newly established Chepstow Cricket Club. With Col Thomas Lewis as its President, the Rev T A Mathews as its Secretary and Sir Edm Williams among its members[27], this was no organisation for the agricultural labourers who characterise Chepstow's Census of Population return and whose weekly wage would have been very little above the half-guinea annual subscription. The local press referred to cricket as being a "fashionable and popular sport"[28] and, among the peripherals of the earliest Chepstow-Monmouth matches, mentions equipages conveying the fairest inhabitants to the ground and an after-match dinner comprising two haunches of venison, turbot, salmon, sherry, port and claret.[29]

---

[21] *The Stranger's Illustrated Guide to Chepstow and its Neighbourhood (1853)* p 14
[22] Lascelles and Co *Gazetteer of the Counties of Monmouth and Hereford 1852* p 46
[23] Ivor Waters *The Town of Chepstow* pp 71-2
[24] Plaque on wall adjacent to Riverside and *Cambridge Biographical Encyclopedia* p 350
[25] Lascelles *Gazetteer* p60
[26] Ib
[27] *Chepstow Cricket Club: The First 150 Years* (ed Alasdair Jacks) p 6
[28] Ib p 4 quoted from *Monmouthshire Merlin* of 25 August 1838
[29] Ib p 5 *Monmouthshire Merlin* 1 September 1838

High standards of behaviour were expected, the Rules and Regulations providing -

7 That any member disputing the decision of an umpire shall pay a fine of five shillings.
8 That any member leaving a game unfinished, unless he shall previous to his being chosen-in state a probability of his being obliged to do so, pay a fine of 2s 6d.
9 That any member, not being actually engaged in a game, standing himself, or whether actually engaged or not, leaving a bat or any part of his dress within forty yards of either of the wickets, shall pay a fine of one shilling.
10 That any member throwing his bat on the ground on leaving the wickets, shall pay a fine of 2s 6d.
11. That upon any impropriety of conduct in any member, the members present shall, at the request of any one member, form themselves into a special committee to enquire into such conduct; and the majority shall expel such member if they think fit[30]

Whether the Club had occasion to implement any of these Rules is not recorded, but they were part of William Pooley's social environment and part of Edward Pooley's family background - respectable, professional, middle-class and above stairs. There is plenty of evidence that Edward was an educated, literate man and it would not have been in the least surprising if his talent for cricket had taken him to one of the universities and into the county side as a gentleman amateur. The reality was rather different.

A common theme of Victorian and early twentieth century fiction and drama is that of the working-class boy or girl made good and from Hamer Shawcross in Howard Spring's *Fame is the Spur*, through Willie Mossop in *Hobson's Choice* and various Catherine Cookson heroes and heroines to Joe Lampton in *Room at the Top*, the tale is one of upward social mobility.

Edward Pooley's story is the reverse of that, from respectable middle-class, through the hero-worship of the Kennington Oval crowds, albeit endowed with a temperament that brought him into clashes with authority, both in the world of cricket and the world outside, to the squandering of a significant benefit fund, rejection by his family and degeneration into poverty and the ignominy of the workhouse. In a way, the middle-class ethos remains with him throughout his life in that all his ten children are given at least two

---

[30]   Ib   p 7

28

names, as were four of his six siblings. He himself had two and while both are present on his birth and marriage certificates, the birth certificates of his first two daughters and that Post Office London Directory entry, I have found no record of the *William* being used after that. One forename was generally the norm for those of humbler origins and while the amateurs may be known as H H Stephenson, F P Miller, H D G Leveson-Gower or whatever, the professionals were known formally by their surnames only and informally by a single first name. It was into this latter category that Ted Pooley most easily slips, a social grade or two lower than the two or three-initialled ones, but Ted slips even lower and at the end of his life is at the very bottom of the social heap.

Why?... It is not the purpose of this book to be judgmental, but simply to present facts and contemporary opinion on a man who in the words of his obituary in *Wisden* was "his own enemy" [31]. However, his life and career are inseparable from a class system of which cricket was a microcosm, where amateurs were divided from professionals and where, however benevolent an employer or ex-employer might be, the post-career opportunities of the ex-professional cricketer were less than they are today.

Pullin took a similar line pointing to the differences in education, social surroundings and moral guidance at the turn of the century compared to thirty or forty years earlier, describing Pooley as "a famous old cricketer down on his luck" and pointing to the stark contrast between Pooley's earlier popularity and recent misfortune.[32]

A century on, some ex-pros still have difficulties coming to terms with life after cricket: David Frith's *By His Own Hand* lists some eighty of them who failed to do so and took their own lives - and there have been more since. Pooley came fairly close to suicide: his contemporary Richard Humphrey took the ultimate step and was found drowned in the Thames in 1906.

Among his 'faults of private character' [33] was one which in modern terms would be described as an addiction to gambling. It was acquired at an early age: as a boy, he had developed a taste for playing cricket on Richmond

---

[31] 1908 Edition p 149
[32] Pullin *Talks with Old English Cricketers* p 132
[33] *Wisden 1908* p 149

Green for stakes of half-a-crown, money which, he says, sometimes took a week or ten days to collect. He was later to play on the same green for £5 a match, his usual match fee as a professional cricketer.[34]

"Before us stands yesterday," said Ted Hughes and if the Child is father of the Man, if "in my end is my beginning", then the gambling instinct was to stay with him throughout his cricketing and post-cricketing life and was to accelerate his decline into pauperdom and penniless death in the workhouse infirmary.

In part, he was a victim of a class divide epitomised in cricket but, in addition, there are vital clues in that previously unexplored Census entry of 1841 and in the ghost of his hitherto unknown elder brother. Child deaths were not uncommon in Victorian Britain, but who can guess the devastating effect of losing a child of three who was just beginning to develop a personality? The family left Chepstow shortly afterwards. Apart from revealing it to the Census Enumerator, did they shut it out from their minds that they had ever been there? Was young Edward resented for not being Thomas? Was he mollycoddled and over-protected? Apart from his father, Edward's family environment was entirely feminine - four sisters, mother, grandmother and maiden aunt - and by the time he was 23, he was to add to those a wife and two baby daughters. Already ten years old by the time Frederick was born, had Edward already begun to develop that Maverick approach to life, that rebellious streak and fiery temper, to reject the nurturing, feminine world of his boyhood and to replace it with the rougher, macho world of professional sport, drinking, gambling and fighting?

Married in 1863 and living with someone else only ten years later was not the kind of role model lifestyle generally admired by Queen Victoria's subjects. The influences of heredity and environment will vary from person to person and the relative importance of professional cricket, nineteenth century class divisions and reaction against a feminine middle-class home background on the life of Edward William Pooley must remain a matter for speculation.

---

[34] Pullin *Talks with Old English Cricketers* p 132

CHAPTER 2

SURREY COLT
(1861/63)

Fund-raising encounters on Richmond Green notwithstanding, Pooley's first organised cricket was with the East Surrey Club whose meetings were held at the Rosemary Branch Tavern in Peckham[35] and as an engaged professional in Perth[36].

His first recorded appearance at the Kennington Oval on which he was to hone his skills and entertain the public for the next two decades and more was on 3 and 4 May 1861, for the Colts against the Gentlemen of the Surrey Club. He was, we now know, 19 at the time though possibly masquerading as 18. He is recorded as 'E Pooley (Richmond)',was bowled by F P Miller in the first innings for 3 and c Bruce b Hayes 0 in the second. A not particularly distinguished match is completed by 16 balls for seven runs in the first innings and a catch in the second. In another account, says Haygarth, the score differs in the second innings of the Colts. Not too much can be read into that, however; nineteenth-century scoring was even more amateurish than it is now and inaccuracies and inconsistencies are manifold.[37]

Nineteenth-century cricket, of course, reflects the class divisions of nineteenth-century society and the distinctions drawn in the nomenclature of teams appearing under the general umbrella of Surrey County Cricket Club - e g Surrey, Gentlemen of Surrey, Players of Surrey and Colts - are not accidental and have a social and cricketing significance.

By 1861 Surrey had become an important part of the cricket scene, threatening the pre-eminence of the MCC and Lord's. Established in 1845, the Kennington-based club was an amalgam of town-based sides and between 1856 and 1859 had won 26 of 29 matches. In 1858 they had beaten a strong England Eleven and taken the decision to build a new pavilion.

---

[35] *S & B* Vol VIII p 430
[36] Pullin *Talks with Old English Cricketers* p 133
[37] *S & B* Vol VII p 13

Among the leading lights of the time were F P Miller, H H Stephenson, William Caffyn and Julius Caesar.[38]

Ten days after playing for the Colts, Pooley made another appearance, this time for the Players of Surrey against Fourteen Gentlemen of the Club on 13 and 14 May 1861. Batting at no 3, he made 26 in the first innings and a duck in the second, took no catches and did not bowl in a match which the Players won by 7 wickets.

Apart from the personal significance of the match for Pooley, it was memorable for a further, if idiosyncratic, reason. Haygarth reports:

In the first innings of the Gentlemen of the Surrey Club, the first four wickets had fallen when it was discovered by Mr John Walker that the match was being played on wickets pitched four feet short. This was soon rectified; but perhaps the game ought to have been recommenced, inasmuch as the first four were lowered when the rules of the game were not being carried out.[39]

The nineteenth-century cricket season tended to start later than it does today and both these matches should perhaps be seen as pre-season warm-ups, the equivalent of which would not appear in the official annals of the game. After these matches Pooley took himself off to Scotland to an engagement as professional to the Perth Cricket Club. He had been recommended by John Lillywhite as a replacement for Chatterton on the strength of his performance for the Colts and his bowling with Lillywhite at Harrow School where he "gave satisfaction". He was signed as a bowler for a period of seven weeks at the rate of £2 per week, plus travelling expenses - a total cost to the Club of £20 which was raised by special subscription. William Sievwright's manuscript *History of Perth Cricket Club* goes on to record

It need hardly be mentioned that since then he has figured very prominently in the cricket world especially as wicket-keeper to the U.S. of England Eleven. [40]

Only four matches were played, against the Stirling Club, the Albion Club of Perth and two against the Caledonian Club of Glasgow. The Perth Club at the time was emerging from a period of relative inactivity and in the first of the two clashes with the Glasgow Club, insisted on playing their

[38]   Eric Midwinter *Darling Old Oval* p 9
[39]   *S & B* Vol VII p 20
[40]   Perth Museum and Art Gallery Archive 479

professional, a practice contrary to the tradition of their opponents who had a rule which provided that they and their opponents should play their matches without the aid of their "trainer". In deference to the wishes of the Perth Club, they made an exception and Pooley, opening the bowling, took 2 for 15 in 50 balls in a match which Perth won by 41 runs.

Scottish newspapers at the time had little cricket coverage, preferring to concentrate on agricultural shows, the laying of the foundation stone for the Wallace monument and the weather, which seems to have been particularly bad, even by Scottish standards:

We still have daily rains here, more or less continued, but never we think an entire dry day. Thick fogs also are frequent and the weather is considered ominous for the potato crop, which is giving way in several localities, and also disastrous for the heavier description of cereals.[41]

Pooley's first-class debut (although the concept of first-class was applied retrospectively, having no currency at the time) was against Kent at The Oval on 19 and 20 August 1861 Surrey lost by seven wickets, having "followed their innings" (compulsory at the time for a deficit of 80 or more) 93 runs behind. Batting at no 10 (Julius Caesar had injured a foot and did not bat, otherwise the debutant would doubtless have been no 11), the young Edward made four in the first innings before being bowled by Edgar Willsher whom seven years later he was to accompany on a tour of Canada and the USA.
The *Sporting Life* recorded that:

Young Pooley the Colt played in this match instead of Sewell....
The colt "Pooley", quite a young un, then joined Mortlock and Pooley made a neat cut for two and a pretty draw for two from Willsher when the latter mercilessly bowled him"[42]

A spirited innings one place higher in the order in the follow on, however, ensured Kent had to bat a second time and won some admiration from the contemporary press.
"A young and most promising county man" said *Bell's Life*.[43] "Pooley, a 'colt' batted with excellent judgment and carried out his bat with 15. He

[41] *Glasgow Herald* 12 August 1861
[42] 21 August 1861
[43] 25 August 1861

will become for a certainty a good acquisition for his county" was the confident and accurate prediction of *The Times* [44]

"Pooley then faced[45] Mr Miller, who made 11, and was then caught at point (eight for 86) and then (Caesar still unable to play) the last man Mudie joined the Colt and "how" the two did hit: the "Young 'Un" made a fine leg hit for 4 from Bennett, a 3, three 2's and two singles....Pooley carried his bat for 15 amid general applause. His free hearty style of hitting took wonderfully with the lookers-on; he is a very promising cricketer, but must recollect that practice alone makes the thorough cricketer" [46]

Injuries, unavailability and Pooley's performance against Kent ensured he retained his place for the second match of the week against The North on the Broughton Ground in Manchester. Not surprisingly for Manchester, the first day was washed out and there was insufficient time for a result. Promoted to open the innings, Edward recorded his first first-class duck. He had, however, already begun to make an impression.

A generation later, William Caffyn recalls:

Ted Pooley played for us in this match. He was afterwards one of the best wicket-keepers ever known, and a fine vigorous bat too. If he had had less wicket-keeping to do he would, in my opinion, have been more to the front as a batsman. He had a lively style of play which somewhat reminded one of Julius Caesar.[47]

So much of an impact had he made that he was invited to accompany H H Stephenson's side for the 1861/62 tour of Australia. Although referred to as an 'England' tour, (The first Test Match - and even that was only retrospectively regarded as such - was still more than a decade away) the party was heavily weighted in favour of Surrey and indeed spawned a "supplementary match", The World (in Australia) v Surrey (in Australia). Even so, it must have been unusual for a soi-disant 18 year-old to have been considered. Haygarth reports that several of the cracks of England were asked to go but would not agree to the terms of £150 and all expenses paid. The party left on 20 October and arrived in Melbourne on Christmas Eve.[48]

---

[44] 21 August 1861.
[45] 'faced' in 19th century reporting means not 'faced the bowling of', but 'was in batting partnership with'
[46] *Sporting Life* 21 August 1861
[47] *Seventy-one Not Out: the reminiscences of William Caffyn* p 166
[48] *S & B* Vol VII pp 197, 213

Pooley was not with them. The financial terms were possibly more of an inducement to him than some of the hardened pros, but there were other reasons for his declining the invitation, which were perhaps not inconsistent with the *Sporting Life*'s mild hint that his approach was not quite 100% professional: forty years on, he admitted to having been involved in a spot of "sweethearting".[49] It is not unlikely that the object of his affections was Ellen Hunt, later to become his bride and the mother of two daughters in what was to be a fairly short-lived marriage.

He had, however, made sufficient of an impression in 1861 to be complimented in the 16th Edition of Lillywhite's *Guide to Cricketers*, which describes Poolley [sic] as a promising player for the county, who batted well and was an excellent field, and to be appointed as a bowler of the club in 1862, a year in which he made eight first-class appearances. Thomas Humphrey and Henry Jupp with whom Pooley was to form an invincible single-wicket combination were also first contracted in that year. Although appointed as a bowler, Pooley did no bowling at all and indeed very little throughout his career. Not that that should be regarded as unusual; all professionals in those days and much later (Hobbs was first appointed as a bowler) were appointed as such, their main function being to bowl at the members in the nets even if their specialism lay in another direction. In statistical terms, it was not the most successful of seasons. In twelve innings, he made 75 at an average of 8.33; but Lillywhite continues to record him as a promising cricketer, describing Pooley (now spelt correctly) as a player who with some little more steadiness, would no doubt appear more prominently in his county's scoring-book, "a good field, an excellent bat, and takes long-leg first-rate"[50]

No mention yet of wicket-keeping, though 1862 did see his introduction to the art. In a non-first-class match for Eleven Surrey players against Twenty Two "Gentlemen" of "Pall Mall", a match in which few of the 'cracks' played,[51] he stumped two in the first innings, so he is being a little economical with the truth in his 'Old Ebor' interview when he tells the Surrey captain in 1863 that he has never kept wicket before![52]

[49] Pullin *Talks with Old English Cricketers* p 133
[50] Frederick Lillywhite's *Guide to Cricketers* (18th Edition) 1863 p 92
[51] *S & B* Vol VII pp 421
[52] Pullin *Talks with Old English Cricketers* p 133

Having gained some experience in less serious cricket, Pooley now turned his attention to the area where he was to dominate the cricket world for the next two decades The story is told in the 'Old Ebor' interview and the Editor of *Wisden* was sufficiently impressed by its importance to consider quoting it verbatim in Pooley's Obituary.

Pooley described how he saw himself as a useful batsman and fielder and occasional right-arm lob bowler, who volunteered to keep wicket when Tom Lockyer, Surrey's regular practitioner since 1849, was injured. Captain F P Miller asked whether Pooley had kept wicket before. He said he hadn't, but H H Stephenson persuaded him to "Let the young 'un have a go." Pooley got a few wickets. Lockyer was delighted and predicted that the "young 'un" would be his successor in the Surrey team.[53]

The accuracy of the anecdote can be questioned: for a start it is being related almost forty years later and it can be safely assumed that it is not a verbatim account of the three-way conversation; secondly, the evidence is that Pooley had kept wicket before and, thirdly, F P Miller had not been captain of Surrey since 1857 and did not play in the match in question which must have been the one against Kent at The Oval on July 16 17 and 18 1863. H H Stephenson played and, as indicated in his invitation to Pooley to tour Australia a couple of years earlier, was clearly an admirer and possibly a mentor of the young pro. In the first innings, Lockyer had a catch and a stumping and Pooley had a catch and the positions were reversed in the second, when Pooley had a catch and a stumping and Lockyer had a catch and also bowled 15 overs.

So Edward Pooley's career as a first-class wicket-keeper was off the ground, the first of his 358 stumping victims being the Kent opener, G M Kelson for a career-best 122. The youngster played two other first-class matches that year, but gained no more victims and finished with a batting average of 8.8 in five innings.

His request to keep wicket was perhaps a plea to be allowed to do something other than make up the numbers. His bowling clearly was not taken seriously and - if we are to assume the batting lists of contemporary

---

[53]   Ib

records actually represent the batting order (they may not, as at times batsmen were listed in social seniority) - he couldn't have been too enthused about batting at 11 as he did against Kent and Yorkshire.

For the first part of the 1863 season he had clearly been playing elsewhere (possibly Perth again) and did not make his first appearance until 29 June against Eighteen of Rugby, Cheltenham and Marlborough Schools. It was, according to Haygarth, "entirely a novel match, never having been played before or since"[54] His performance was undistinguished. Batting at 10, he made a "pair", run out in the first innings, bowled in the second.

His loyalty to the club may have been somewhat diluted and he was less than enthusiastic about committing himself to minor matches. Haygarth records[55] that "the players were disappointed of Jupp, Pooley and others" for A Scratch Eleven of Players from the Oval against a Scratch Twenty-two of the Civil Service Club with their bowler, Broomfield, in Battersea Park on 14 August.

This is not the only instance of lack of commitment and organisation by Surrey and its representatives in 1863. When the Gentlemen of Manchester arrived at The Oval on 25 May for a fixture with the Gentlemen of Surrey, they were "astounded" to find that no match would take place as their putative opponents had taken themselves off to Lord's to watch the United England XI play the All England XI.[56] And later in the year, against Southgate, Lockyer, now very obviously in the twilight of his career declined to play unless the umpire were replaced. The umpire was not replaced and Lockyer did not play.[57]

By the end of that season, however, Lockyer's eventual successor had begun to take his talents elsewhere and in early September turned out for Twenty-two of the Middlesex clubs [sic - the Middlesex *Club* was not formed until the following year] against the United England Eleven, scored a few and stumped John Lillywhite. It was to Middlesex that Pooley was to transfer his allegiance the following year.

---

[54] S & B Vol VIII p 88
[55]   Ib   p 168
[56]   Ib   p 164
[57]   Ib   p 196

His decision may have been not entirely unconnected with finance: he now had a wife to support. He had married Ellen Hunt on 25 March 1863 and their first child would be born the following January. The marriage took place in St Peter's Church, Walworth, where Edward's father William and younger sister Irene were witnesses. Ellen was at the time 24: Edward is recorded on the certificate as 22, though he was in fact just over 21, an indication that he was as capable of adding a year to reduce the age-gap between himself and his wife, as he was of deducting a year to improve his chances of succeeding as a professional cricketer. Interestingly, he was perhaps not so confident at this time about his future career and describes himself on the marriage certificate as a tobacconist.

CHAPTER 3

MIDDLESEX ETC
(1864/65)

Whether it was disenchantment with Surrey, the attraction of a new start with a newly-formed county club or his new domestic responsibilities is unclear and Pooley claims not to be able to remember[58] but the beginning of 1864, the year in which the first edition of *Wisden* appeared and overarm bowling was legalised, saw him living in Islington and trying his luck across the river. His selective amnesia may owe much to what turned out to be a brief marriage to Ellen Hunt and the subsequent birth of two daughters, Ellen Harriett Eliza (her first two names after her mother and grandmother and her third probably after her aunt) in 1864 and Fanny Maria the following year. Edward and Ellen had begun married life in Amelia Road, Newington, within easy reach of the Kennington Oval and very close to the Renfrew Road Workhouse where he was to end his days.

Regulations on qualification for a particular county by birth or residence were not yet firmly in place and - as we shall see later with James Southerton who has the distinction of having played for three counties in the same season - arrangements were much more flexible than they were subsequently to become.

Not that the set-up, such as it was, was without criticism. In *The Walkers of Southgate*, W A Bettesworth[59] mentions that the composition of the Middlesex team for the match against Sussex at Islington, the first match on the new Middlesex Ground, adjacent to the cattle market at Islington, roused the indignation of one of the sporting papers of the day.

It was a scratch team for Wells, though born in London, lived all his life, except a few days, in Sussex, and always played for the county when not opposed to Middlesex, which then claimed him - birth then counting, unfairly perhaps in some cases, before residence. The two Hearnes, Tom and George, were born in Buckinghamshire, Mr Case in Lancashire, Mr J J Sewell in Gloucestershire, E Pooley in Surrey, Mr Tritton in Surrey, Mr B B Cooper in India.

---

[58]   Pullin *Talks with Old English Cricketers* p133
[59]   pp 284-5

Bettesworth had commented earlier[60] that "It is a little startling to find Pooley making 53 on the side of Southgate". With a wife and infant daughter to support, the young professional was doubtless looking to make whatever he could from the game . The occasion was a twelve-a-side match against Surrey on 25 and 26 August and for Pooley, it appears to have been almost a one-off (He did play for Southgate as a "given man" against the Surrey Club in June 1865), but as well as his half-century, he distinguished himself with four catches and a couple of stumpings.

Despite not being engaged for Surrey for the 1864 season[61], the Surrey allegiance was not severed entirely and Pooley did play at The Oval in September for Eleven Surrey Players with Pryor against Sixteen Gentlemen of the Surrey Club. He did a spot of bowling, took three wickets in the first innings, four in the second. But it does not seem to have been too serious an occasion. Haygarth reports[62] that the match was played for the benefit of the nine Surrey bowlers engaged this season at The Oval. None of the best Surrey gentlemen seems to have played for the Sixteen, and the match was devoid of all interest. It was unfinished with the Players at 38-2 requiring but two runs to win.

The following month, on 12 and 13 October (the cricket season at this time was ill defined, but tended to be June to October), he was one of "Three Surrey Players" who played against "An Eleven" on the Middlesex County Ground at Islington but, according to Haygarth, it was a fairly meaningless encounter.[63]

In this match it must be remembered that the Three Surrey Players had the privilege of hitting all round, whilst the Eleven were restricted to making their hits before the wicket and behind the crease, otherwise their total had been nearer 200 than 62. These kinds of matches, however, are meaningless and unsatisfactory, and cannot be considered as having any legitimate title or claim to public support being usually promoted either for gambling purposes, gate money or the gratification of personal vanity...

Single-wicket was a variety of the game where there was only one set of stumps, a single stump at the other end of the pitch from which the ball was bowled. Only one batsman was in at any given time. The game could be

---

[60]   Ib p 235
[61]   *S & B* Vol VIII p 293
[62]   Ib p 516
[63]   Ib p 539

played between teams of varying sizes but when there were fewer than five in the field, scoring strokes could be made only in front of the wicket and byes, overthrows, catches behind the wicket and stumpings were not allowed.[64]

Pooley was now getting well established on the professional cricket circuit: as well as the single wicket stuff, benefit matches and matches against the odds, he involved himself with the "New All England XI" which had an extremely brief life-span, its existence beginning with a match against Twenty-two of Oxford and District on the new Christchurch ground at Oxford on 23, 24 and 25 June and ending on 27, 28 and 29 June against Eighteen of Sheffield at Hyde Park in that city, a match played for the benefit of the "Sheffield inundation fund". The New All England Eleven lost by an innings and 32 runs and never played again!

The new team was, says Haygarth,

it is believed an amalgamation of T Sherman's and F Caesar's Elevens. The Eleven, however, was, it seems, not well managed and kept together, for they only played two matches, and broke up at the end of the season. Secretary (it is believed) E Pooley, but no account could be obtained for insertion.[65].

Subsequent research[66] suggests that this was in fact the *fourth* New All England Eleven. The first two were established in 1858, the more significant one by Thomas Sherman and Frank Chadband, but the team failed to attract opposition and collapsed. A parallel side was established by Fred Caesar, brother of Julius. This too survived one season, but re-emerged in 1862 as 'Another' New All England XI. It was to this team that Pooley was attached, but his presence failed to win any of their five matches. In September of that year Sherman's lot played Caesar's lot for the right to style themselves the New All England XI. Caesar's XI won, but neither side appeared again. Pooley's main recollection is that "the money was divided - and there was a rare bother over the division"[67] Undeterred, Pooley formed his team which, though it never played again, became an antecedent of the United South of England XI which was to be the longest lived of the touring sides of the nineteenth century, surviving until 1882. Its

---

[64] Michael Rundell *The Dictionary of Cricket* p 214
[65] Ib p 353
[66] Ric Sissons *The Players* pp 61-63
[67] Pullin *Talks with Old English Cricketers* p140

success and longevity were not entirely unconnected with the presence of the "amateur " W G Grace who took over the team which was to be his main source of income until he qualified as a doctor in 1879.[68]

Pooley's first appearance at Lord's - the benchmark for a biography in Haygarth's *Scores and Biographies* - was on July 25 and 26 1864 for Middlesex against MCC and Ground and was distinguished by Middlesex being dismissed for 20, still their lowest score in first-class cricket. MCC eventually won by 5 wickets, Pooley was c and b Wootton 0 in the first innings and in the second, more euphonically , c Sutton b Wootton 10.

Notwithstanding that undistinguished appearance at the game's headquarters, however, 1864 was his best season in first-class cricket so far. He scored 188 runs at 13.42, stumped nine and caught eight, but the records are not sufficiently accurate to say whether all those were as wicket-keeper. His Middlesex statistics - not all first-class - are given as 8 matches, 11 innings, 173 runs, highest score 43 (v Bucks at Newport Pagnell - not first class) , average 15.8[69]. W J Ford, however, writing more than 30 years later when the accuracy of statistics was beginning to be more significant, comments under 'Wicket-keeping':-

Statistics impossible, from lack of information The gloves often seem to have been passed from one man to another, so that it is impossible to say whether catches were made in the field or at the wicket. It is better to give no details at all than those which are purely conjectural.[70]

Lillywhite, however, with the immediacy of the eye-witness not available to Ford seems to be more confident that Pooley was Middlesex's regular keeper and writes:

Pooley kept wicket in all eight County matches (except in the first innings at Lord's when Mr Nicholson was behind). In these 8 matches Pooley stumped 10 and caught out 10, averaging 2 per match and 4 over, a highly commendable performance; he also stumped and caught out one in the match against the Knickerbockers.

In reviewing Pooley's season in more general terms, he begins to wax lyrical :

---

[68] .Robert Low *W G* p 101
[69] 15 and "8 over", decimal fractions not being used until later in the century
[70] p 28

One approaching, and very soon to be an 'A.1'. A splendid wicket-keeper, beautiful bat, and a good change-bowler, therefore useful in any eleven. Plays for Surrey (born) and Middlesex (residence), on which ground he is engaged.[71]

It was about this time that, according to Haygarth, Pooley took on a "cricket and cigar store" at 2 Barford Terrace, Liverpool Road, Islington.[72] It was here that his daughter Ellen was born. The shop receives no mention in the Post Office London Directory for 1865, but there was a tobacconist there in 1864, the premises having been unoccupied in 1863 - one Charles William Cope[73] who is not recorded the following year. By early 1864, Pooley had taken over the business[74] and the *Cricketers' Companion* records that he lives near the new Middlesex Cricket Ground[75], which at the time was behind the cattle market in Caledonian Road, a very short distance away. It seems, in any case, to have been a short-lived venture, for the following year he was back across the river and fully committed to Surrey.

The shop was one of a block of four with living accommodation above in a respectable middle-class district. It was, ironically in view of the way Pooley's life was to end, occupied in 1861[76] by a Clerk to the Poor Law Board, his wife, three children and servant. No 1 was a coffee and chop-house and no 3 a millinery ; like Pooley's, both ventures seem to be of short duration; by 1866, no 1 was an Italian warehouse and no 3 a bookbindery. A William Fordham (profession unspecified) is listed under no 2. By 1870, Post Office reorganisation had resulted in 1,2 and 3 Barford Terrace becoming 70, 72 and 74 Liverpool Road and the demography had again moved on. They were then occupied by a printer, a chemist and dressmaker. No 4 (now 76) was the premises of an auctioneer and furniture dealer. Constant throughout all these fluctuations was the White Horse (still there, but now The Islington Tup) and its publican, Thomas Cooke. Between the shops and the pub was the London Fever Hospital, later the Royal Free Hospital and now up-market residential accommodation, as Islington becomes once again a fashionable part of London. Pooley's old shop, now 72 Liverpool Road, is half of a Tandoori Restaurant.

---

[71] Frederick Lillywhite's *Guide to Cricketers* 20th Edition 1864 p 119
[72] *S & B* Vol VIII p 430
[73] *Post Office London Directory* 1864 edition p493
[74] On his marriage certificate and his daughter Ellen's birth certificate, his occupation is recorded as 'Tobacconist'
[75] *Cricketers' Companion* 1865 p 119
[76] 1861 Census of Population

Parallel to all this and not noted by Haygarth or any one else, as far as I can ascertain, is a record in the same series of Post Office London Directories for 1863 to 1865[77] of Edward William Pooley operating as a tobacconist, but at a shop at the junction of Old Ford Road and Park Road in Bow - now disappeared under the A102(M) and very near to the "Home in the East for the Reformation of Criminal Boys". In 1866, the business was taken over by Charles Horwood and in 1867 by Mrs Frances Ward.

The strong likelihood is that this Edward William Pooley (apart from his own birth and marriage certificates and his children's birth certificates, the only instance of the *William* I have come across) is our man: the time he is there coincides with the time when his links with Surrey are looser and we know there is a family connection with the East End, his parents having been married in Stepney. He was involved with the Peckham-based East Surrey club, his father died in Mile End and his brother later lived and died in East Ham. It seems highly unlikely that Pooley would have been able to devote sufficient attention to the business in the summer months to make it viable and it is perhaps unsurprising that his little business venture ceased when he resumed seriously with Surrey in 1866. It is of passing interest perhaps that Pooley had two attempts at entrepreneurship - one with tobacco and one with alcohol !

In 1865 however, Pooley played only once for Middlesex, against Hampshire for which county his future ally Southerton made one of his thirteen appearances and ironically had him stumped. Then once again, he threw in his lot with Surrey, mainly, says Ford[78] as a batsman, but partly as understudy to Lockyer who, now in his penultimate season, was often called upon to bowl. Pooley had a recollection of being "fetched back" by the Surrey secretary[79].

The switch seems to have been fairly early in the season; by May, he was in the newly established United South of England Eleven, by mid-June, in the Surrey side at Bramall Lane and playing regularly for them after that, including the matches against Middlesex at The Oval in July and back at Islington, in August. It was between playing his last match for Middlesex

[77] see Note 4
[78] W J Ford *Middlesex County Cricket Club 1864-99* p 38
[79] Pullin *Talks with Old English Cricketers* p 133

against Hampshire and rejoining Surrey in Sheffield that his second daughter, Fanny Maria (the second name probably after Pooley's elder sister) was born on 14 June 1865. What happened to Ellen and whether there were subsequent children I have been unable to discover, but it seems likely that at some stage over the next seven or eight years, she and Edward separated. Unusually, however, Ellen and Fanny stayed not with their mother, but with their father who seemed to get help from his own mother with their upbringing.

1865 seems to have been something of a fragmented year for Pooley. As well as his tobacconist's business, his fatherhood, his fluctuation between Surrey and Middlesex and his involvement with the newly established United South of England XI, early in the season he took an engagement in Northern Ireland as Lord Massereene's private professional.

The season seems to have begun a little earlier on the other side of the Irish Sea and Easter Saturday, 15 April, saw Pooley and Tom Heighes, the North of Ireland professional, playing for the Next Sixteen against the First Eleven of the North of Ireland Club in an early season trial match. The local press commented that it showed the vitality of the club and the increasing interest taken in the 'noble game' for it to turn out an Eleven and a Sixteen so early in the season and was delighted that "a few ladies graced the scene with their presence".

The match itself is reported on at some length and international news reduced to a footnote below the scorecard:

Assaults and robberies are becoming very prevalent in Jamaica.
The Russian Government has removed the restrictions on public smoking, and smokers can now enjoy the weed while passing along the streets.
On Good Friday the London Crystal Palace was the scene of a grand musical entertainment. About 40,000 visitors were present.
The Viceroy of Egypt has shut himself in a fort at the mouth of the Nile until his astrologers, by consulting the stars, can ascertain whether the Viceroy may undertake a long contemplated journey to France and England[80]

Without troubling to consult the stars, Pooley played a few matches for Lord Massereene's XI and also turned out as a professional for the Garrison team against the North of Ireland Club, distinguishing himself as a bowler taking

---

[80] *Belfast Newsletter* 19 April 1865

six wickets in the first innings and three in the second, including his Lordship on both occasions. No bowling analysis was kept (not unusual at the time) though Pooley and Heighes seem to have been the only bowlers used and the local newspaper reported that "the bowling of Pooley and Heighes for the garrison…was first-rate"[81] Pooley was top-scorer in each of the Garrison's innings and contributed substantially to a 45-run victory.

It all seems to have been fairly sociable stuff, the band of the 97th regiment playing each day by permission of the colonel and officers of the depot[82], and when Lord Massereene entertained visiting sides at his "beautiful and picturesque ground at Antrim Castle", "luncheon was served up in the Castle in a princely style".[83] On another occasion "The West-End Eleven were entertained at luncheon by Lord Massereene in his usual sumptuous and liberal manner and they felt it only incumbent upon them to thank his lordship most warmly for the hospitable style in which they were treated and the delightful day's cricket he afforded them"[84]. Being required to bowl - and the *Belfast Newsletter* refers to "the capital bowling of the professional Pooley"- he did not keep wicket. That was his Lordship's prerogative.

His bowling skills were less exercised when he returned to England and cricket of a more professional and competitive kind with Surrey and the United South of England XI which had been formed the previous November, following acrimony in the three North v South fixtures and the refusal of twelve southern players to play in the fourth at Newmarket.[85] It was one of three professional touring XIs (the others being the northern-based All-England XI and Midlands-orientated United England XI).

Most of its games were against "Twenty-twos" - the first against 22 of Ireland in Dublin. Pooley did not play in that one, being still engaged in the north of the same country at the time, but made his début on 25 May at Pleasington, near Blackburn against Twenty-two of Pleasington with John Smith (of Yeadon) and Darnton. The USEE played fourteen matches in their inaugural season, including appearances at delightfully named locations, like the Dripping Pan, Lewes, Lower Mitcham Green and Broadwater, near Godalming. Pooley played in eight, sometimes keeping

[81] Ib   22 May 1865
[82] Ib
[83] Ib   20 May 1865
[84] Ib   24 May 1865
[85] Sissons *The Players* p 59

wicket and regularly batting at no 3. One of his less distinguished performances was to be in the middle of a hat-trick against Twenty-two of St Albans, when "Hughes, with the first three balls he delivered, got out Humphrey, Pooley, and Jupp; a great feat. "[86]

After Pooley's solitary match for Middlesex on 1 and 2 June and an appearance for "Southgate with Pooley" against the Surrey Club on 12 and 13 June and the birth of his second daughter, he played regularly for Surrey, dividing the rest of the season between his supposed native county and the USEE. Tom Lockyer was coming to the end of a distinguished career as a middle-order batsman, fast-medium round arm bowler and wicket-keeper, the latter duties shared in 1865 with the emerging Edward Pooley, who was clearly good enough to hold a place on his batting alone, recording 82 not out against Kent, his highest first-class score so far and averaging 20.38 in first-class matches. Trans-century statistical comparisons are not very meaningful because of variations in the standard of pitches but, if we look at what typical averages were at the time, a rough 20th century equivalent would be not far off 40, good enough to hold down a place in most county sides.

Acrimony between north and south has traditionally been a feature not only of English cricket, but of English life and that summer hostilities were at their height. There was a background of anti-Surrey feeling which had its roots in the no-balling of Edgar Willsher in the Surrey v England match at The Oval in 1862, the umpire John Lillywhite taking the view that he had raised his arm above the shoulder, illegal at the time, and there was a strong suspicion that Lillywhite was acting on the instructions of the Surrey authorities. The England professionals walked off and play was not resumed until the following day and then with a replacement umpire[87]. The ill-feeling which followed was instrumental in the schism between northern and southern professionals which led to the fragmentation into three professional touring XIs.

In 1865, five Yorkshire professionals declined to play against Surrey, both at Bramall Lane and The Oval. 'Secessionists' they were dubbed by Haygarth who commented as follows on the Surrey-Yorkshire match at The Oval in August.

---

[86] *S & B* Vol IX p 257
[87] Sissons *The Players* p 56

Altogether this match (as well as others over the last five years at The Oval) was a good deal spoiled by the still continued disputes in the *professional* cricket community. It is much to be regretted that whatever the quarrels between cricketers might be, they should prevent any from assisting their counties. The match was not resumed in 1866 but next came off in 1867.[88]

Relationships with Nottinghamshire were scarcely more harmonious, George Parr and some of his colleagues declining to play in any match which had a Surrey connection. Matters came to a head in The Oval match in 1865 when a questionable run out decision led to a Surrey victory by one wicket.

A decision of the umpire in favour of the batsman gave so much offence (He was out by a yard and a half, Oscroft declared), that the match between the counties ceased until 1868[89]

Having noted that only one amateur participated in the match, Haygarth reported as follows:

In the second innings of Surrey, when the ninth wicket fell, there were wanted 14 runs to get to win, the whole of which were obtained curiously by the last man in, T Sewell.
G Parr refused to play against Surrey, or the result might have been different.
This match was not resumed in 1866, the old grievance having been reopened and the Nottingham players and spectators being greatly dissatisfied with a decision of the umpire towards the conclusion of the above contest. When the Nottinghamshire matches were being arranged for 1866, it was agreed by the committee of Notts and by the professionals themselves that 'if the match could not be played pleasantly, it were better not played at all.'[90]

Nor was crowd behaviour impeccable - even at benefit matches. Towards the end of the season, Eighteen Gentlemen of the Surrey Club (alternatively described as a Gentlemen of the South of England XVIII) played the USEE for the benefit of the ground bowlers at The Oval. There were the usual pleasantries; including the Surrey custom of rewarding any Gentleman who scored 50 with a bat and any professional with a sovereign "talent money", but all was not sweetness and light.

---

[88] *S & B* Vol IX pp 217-8
[89] Rt Hon Lord Alverstone and C W Alcock *Surrey Cricket, its History and Associations* p 84
[90] *S & B* Vol IX p 147

Jupp was playing a typical stonewalling innings in an ultimately unsuccessful attempt to stave off defeat. E M Grace, (W G's elder brother) tried a counter-tactic which did not overimpress the Oval public.

During the game considerable sensation was caused and dissatisfaction expressed at Mr Grace's peculiar and novel bowling to Jupp. The batsman (Jupp) was "pitched out", and loudly called upon by spectators to remain where he was, as they considered it unfair cricket. The kind of ball (very high in the air and falling vertically on the wicket) is probably the most difficult of all to play. It may not be graceful, but (as the law now stands) it is quite fair, there is no doubt. Therefore the cries of 'Shame,' 'Shame," and the hissing which the act caused were quite uncalled for.[91]

Uncalled for or not, the match was held up for an hour and E M and two of his team-mates armed themselves with stumps as improvised weapons for use in combatting what was beginning to look like a riot.[92]

Pooley was not, of course, directly involved in any of the incidents, but he was now five years into his first-class career and still at an impressionable age. There can be no doubt that he was absorbing the culture of a rough, tough professional game in one of its most turbulent periods. So perhaps we have here another influence on the character of the young man (He was 23 during the 1865 season) and the time is not too far ahead when, if ever there is controversy on or off the field, it is a safe bet that he will not be very far away.

Now well established in both the Surrey and USEE, Pooley again rounded off the season with some 'Three of Surrey' matches - firstly against 'Eleven of Richmond' on Richmond Green. The 'Three' were the celebrated Jupp-Pooley-Humphrey combination which Pooley claims was never beaten[93] (and, unlike some of Pooley's statements in that interview, I have no evidence to the contrary). However, Haygarth reported that "the 'Green' even between wickets was very rough and bad, all good play on behalf of the Three being thereby deteriorated."[94]

As we have seen in Chapter 2, Edward Pooley, Henry Jupp and Thomas Humphrey had been simultaneously contracted by Surrey as professional

---

[91]   Ib   pp 292-3
[92]   Low *W G*   p 49
[93]   Pullin *Talks with Old English Cricketers* p 140
[94]   *S & B* Vol IX p 281

cricketers in 1862. Humphrey was the eldest by some three years, Jupp being just three months older than Pooley. All three were to achieve prominent reputations in the English cricket of the 1860s and 1870s, though Pooley was a wicket-keeper who could bat and the other two were specialist batsmen, Humphrey the 'Pocket Hercules', Jupp 'Young Stonewall'. Both died relatively young. Humphrey was not to see his fortieth birthday and Jupp was to die in 1889 at the age of 47.

Following their success on Richmond Green, they played Eleven of the Isle of Thanet and Eleven of Putney and District. In between, they played for Eleven Players of the South against Fourteen Gentlemen of the South, an "inferior lot" according to Haygarth[95] and won by an innings and 179 runs. Jupp scored 216, Pooley 111 and the heatwave continued into October.

It may be remarked that the weather continued hitherto wonderfully fine, brilliant sun, cloudless sky, heat great and no rain had fallen for near two months[96]

For Pooley too, the sun had shone through the summer and Lillywhite's end-of-term report continues his eulogy from the previous year:

The merit of this player was not only alluded to in high terms in the edition of last year's GUIDE, but will also be mentioned in the introduction to the averages of the last season. He is a cricketer all over, quite first-rate as a wicket-keeper, and bat - bar the dropping of his knee to cause a leg before wicket. Good anywhere in the field and an excellent change-bowler.[97]

adding in the introduction to the Averages:

Also Pooley, who has proved himself to be quite at 'the top of the tree' in every department of the game. As a wicket-keeper, he cannot be excelled, in the field anywhere he is at home, and his figures prove what he can do with the bat[98]

[95]   Ib   p 289
[96]   Ib   p 296
[97]   Cricketers' Companion 22nd edition p 153
[98]   Ib   p 39

CHAPTER 4

SURREY PROFESSIONAL, A WORLD RECORD AND THE U S A (1866/68)

Surrey entered 1866 with a truncated fixture list, the matches with Nottinghamshire and Yorkshire having been expunged by the North-South schism, though Lancashire were included for the first time. The modifications were not considered significant by the compilers of the Club's Centenary book who record:

The only important change in the Surrey XI of the year was that Pooley, considered by many to be the greatest of all Surrey "stumpers" had taken Lockyer's place. [99]

Lockyer continued to make the occasional appearance, but mainly as a bowler and 1866 was to be his last season.

Although Pooley's first county engagement had been in 1862, it was not until three years later that his career really took off. He was not re-engaged the following season, went off to play for Middlesex in 1864 and the early part of 1865, and was reclaimed by Surrey when the time had come to replace Tom Lockyer as wicket-keeper.

The remainder of that year had seen Pooley's blossoming as both batsman and wicket-keeper and he was clearly good enough to be selected for his batting alone as demonstrated by his maiden first-class fifty, 82 not out against Kent in July and 59 against England in August, both at The Oval, and although Kent's run of poor form (Surrey won the match by an innings and 98 runs) and the weakening of the England team by the absence of the Northern 'cracks' are both regretted by Haygarth[100], it was as true then as it is now that "You've still got to get 'em".

In fifteen first-class matches in 1866, Pooley had 17 catches and 10 stumpings, including six at Bramall Lane from amateur George Griffith's

---

[99] *Surrey County Cricket Club 1845-1945 Centenary* p 57
[100] *S & B* Vol IX pp 159/60, 232

slow left-handed lobs,[101] an art at which he was later to excel with James Southerton. He was now established on the first-class scene and played in the first two of his 25 Gentlemen v Players matches.

For Surrey the season was less successful than the previous ones; of 13 first-class matches, they lost seven, some by large margins; against England they were hopelessly outclassed, losing by an innings and 296 and scoring only one more run between them in both their innings than the opposing 18-year-old W G Grace (224 not out) had in his - and for good measure, during the course of the match, Grace took himself off to win the 440 yards hurdles at Crystal Palace. At 283-6, in England's mammoth total of 521, "Pooley handed the gloves to Stephenson and went on to bowl."[102]

Haygarth records:

As latterly with Kent, so it was now absurd for Surrey or any other *single* county to continue playing against All England even though (as in this instance) England had not near their best eleven, owing to the continued refusal of the Northern "cracks" to come south, they preferring the Twenty-two matches as being more lucrative.[103]

Three weeks later, as Middlesex amassed a similarly large total -

All the Surrey Eleven were put on to bowl, an event (it is believed) hitherto without a parallel in a great match, and in scarcely any other.[104]

Pooley took one of the half-dozen first class wickets of his career, finishing with 1-50 in 12.2 overs, a caught and bowled, as well as two stumpings, including John Sewell for his career-best 166. Middlesex won by an innings and 70 runs.

Pooley's involvement with the USEE continued: in the match against St Albans his 2nd innings dismissal is idiosyncratically recorded as "picked up ball 4", an entry rivalled perhaps in the match v Peterborough by that relating to E Merrett who, batting at no 17 for Peterborough is "obstructed field, b Bennett 1" Lucky old Bennett!

---

[101] S & B   Ib   p 359
[102] J R Webber *The Chronicle of W G* p 53
[103] S & B Vol IX p 528
[104] S & B   Ib   p 589

A few matches were missed through illness and Pooley stood umpire in others; but, despite failing to record a first-class 50 (He had 49 against Cambridge University when Lillywhite's *Cricketers' Companion* speaks of his "spirited hitting"[105], he was now very much part of the Surrey and USEE scene at a time when cricket was enjoying unprecedented popularity. As late as 8 and 9 October, Eleven Players took on Sixteen of Godalming and Guildford for James Broomfield's benefit and Haygarth comments:

It will be observed that matches containing good names are now played very late in the season. Cricket, however, was now become so common that there was probably no room for an earlier day.[106]

1867 saw more first-class appearances than previously (20), his highest aggregate so far (690), a highest score of 85 for the Players at The Oval, most fifties (five, including two in the same match) but most significantly, more than twice as many dismissals as in any previous season (39 catches and 22 stumpings). In all cricket, Haygarth's potted biography points to a season verging on the phenomenal - 1148 runs and 120 wickets[107].

As always at this period, the statistical accuracy may be questionable, but there is no doubt that Haygarth was impressed and, if nothing else, the figures are indicative of the sheer amount of cricket played.

He produced some outstanding all round performances, including a contribution to a win over his colleagues of three seasons before at Islington. He had three stumpings and four catches in the match, five of the seven dismissals from what Haygarth calls Southerton's *slow* round armed insinuators[108] and then, in the second innings, joined H H Stephenson at 109-5 with a further 71 required to win and with 33 not out steered Surrey to victory. It was the beginning of a fruitful partnership with Southerton who was still dividing his time between Surrey, Hampshire and Sussex and indeed, in the very next match took 12 wickets for Sussex *against* Surrey at Brighton.

On 1,2 and 3 August Pooley and Southerton teamed up again, this time for the USEE against Mr John Walker's Fifteen of Southgate. Pooley had

---

[105] *Cricketers' Companion* 1867 23rd Edition p 167
[106] *S & B* Vol IX p 647
[107] Ib Vol VIII p 430
[108] *S & B* Vol IX p 189/90

seven victims (six in conjunction with Southerton). In Southgate's second innings, Southerton mesmerised a Mr Daniel to the extent that he failed to lay a bat on any one of fifteen consecutive balls.[109] The intervention of the wicket-keeper then saved the hapless Mr Daniel from further punishment - st Pooley b Southerton 0.

Overall, however, the professionals cut matters pretty fine in this fixture and were indebted to Pooley for their emergence from it with dignity and respectability intact -

...but for Pooley and Tom Hearne, who had played so much at Southgate that he knew the bowling of the Walkers pretty thoroughly, the South would not have cut a very good figure.[110]

In addition to his wicket-keeping victims, Pooley had 57 and 14 with the bat and continued to entertain The Oval crowds with his batting. In the return match against Sussex at The Oval which Surrey won by 71 runs, he scored a half-century in each innings including a hit to leg from Southerton which, "bounding over the paling, went as far as Clayton Street."[111]

Late in the season, a benefit match was played for him on Richmond Green between USEE (hyperbolically exaggerated to 'Eleven of England' in the local press) and 22 of the Richmond Town Club. It appears that there was some quality batting on the first day and second morning, but then 'dinner' or, more likely, whatever was taken with it, seems to have had its effect:

A match for the benefit of Pooley, a native of Richmond, and who is now one of the most prominent members of the Surrey eleven was played on the Green on Monday and two following days. Unlike most of the "England" elevens that play in this kind of match, the team which came to battle against twice their number, was a strong one and included some of the best professional cricketers to be found. Some of them showed their skill to some purpose, as the state of the score on Monday night showed - 231 runs and only one wicket down. A cheerful prospect for the 22 certainly; they went at it again the next morning but could not effect a parting until after dinner and then batting seemed to fall off - the eye was not quite so steady - and the bowling apparently improved. Payne was at last got rid of; he was the only one clean bowled. The others were then disposed of quickly and the total reached 309 of the which 306 were made when the second wicket fell. The tired out field then assumed the defensive, but did very little

[109] Ib   Vol X p 217-8
[110] W A Bettesworth *The Walkers of Southgate* p196
[111] S &B Vol X p 261

against the attack of Sewell, Bennett and Lillywhite. The game ended in a draw on Wednesday evening,"[112]

The strength of the Eleven on which the local press comments here can perhaps be seen as a tribute to Pooley's popularity and indicative of the esteem in which he was held by his fellow professionals. Batting at 6, the beneficiary was caught and bowled Walsh for 2 and part of a collapse which was not quite as dramatic as the newspaper suggests. 309 is a misprint for 369!!

The increasing popularity of the game and reputation being established by the USEE, then in its third season, is illustrated by an observation by Haygarth on the inaugural match on the "Hoglands" in Southampton against Eighteen of Hampshire that the Mayor and Corporation walked in procession to the ground and a dinner was given afterwards to the Eleven.[113]

If the professionals continued to be hard-nosed and mercenary, then the amateurs continued to be casual and dilettante and attract some criticism, even from the partisan Haygarth, never slow to highlight the performances of any Harrovians playing in the Middlesex (or any other) side. After enjoying the hospitality at Richmond, the USEE took themselves off to play Twenty-two of the Middlesex Club. "In the second innings of the Eleven, no less [sic] than 9 of the Twenty-two were absent when required to field; such behaviour is not cricket." [114]

The end of the season was again marked by an Eleven versus a Three single wicket contest, this time Eleven of Putney v Pooley, Jupp and Humphrey (Who else?). The three beat the Eleven by an innings and 10 runs - 39 against 9 and 20, Pooley taking ten out of eleven wickets in 213 balls in the first innings and Humphrey emulating even this achievement by taking all eleven in the second in 175.

Notwithstanding his outstanding performance as a bowler against opposition which, with all due respect to the eleven good burghers of Putney, may not have been of the highest quality, the *Cricketers'*

---

[112] *Surrey Comet* 7 September 1867
[113] *S & B* Vol X p 22
[114]   Ib   p 299

Companion continues to record against Pooley's name: "splendid wicket-keeper; very fine batsman"[115]

And so to 1868 and Pooley's World Record. Of all the records listed in *Wisden*, none, other than the highly questionable 'Record Hit' of 1857, stood as long as Pooley's twelve wickets in a first-class match, achieved against Sussex at The Oval on 6 and 7 July 1868. It was equalled twice, by Don Tallon for Queensland against New South Wales at Sydney in 1938/39 and by Brian Taber for New South Wales against South Australia at Adelaide in 1968/69, but not until April 1996 was it beaten - by Wayne James, playing for Matebeleland against Mashonaland Country Districts at the Bulawayo Athletic Club. For good measure, he also captained the side and scored 99 and 99 not out with the bat! Pooley's achievement, however, remains unsurpassed in English first-class cricket. There have been a few 11s, (two by Surrey players - Arnold Long and Alec Stewart) but nothing to equal or beat it.

The following year's *Wisden* makes no mention of a record, but such an omission is scarcely astonishing, since this was only the sixth edition of the Almanack and preceded the time when match reports and season's summaries were included. The only statistical feature was by the Editor and was on *Individual Innings of more than 200 runs*.

Haygarth mentions that it is the largest number *perhaps* (my italics) ever got out by the wicket-keeper in an eleven a side[116] and Lillywhite's *Cricketers' Companion* mentions that

the feature of the match was the wicket-keeping. Pooley caught eight and stumped four, a feat of rare occurrence. [117]

Statistical consciousness was not as acute in 1868 as it became in the following century and although contemporary journalists, compiling the first draft of history, were aware of the unusual nature of the feat, they tended to concentrate more on the quality of the wicket-keeping, rather than the statistical achievement. Certainly, Haygarth had forgotten about it four

---

[115] 1868 edition p 146
[116] *S & B* Vol X p 459
[117] *Cricketers' Companion* 1869 p41

years later when he commented in relation to a performance by the Sussex wicket-keeper that

H Phillips stumped five and caught five which it is believed is the largest number ever got out by a wicket-keeper in an eleven a side match[118]

but then again Haygarth never did have too much time for Pooley's wicket-keeping feats, tending to undermine dismissals from Southerton's "tempting insinuators". In the match in which Pooley established his record, however, Southerton was playing for Sussex and was the twelfth victim.

The Times makes no mention of the possibility of a record, though does say in its report on the first day's play:

Sussex were favourites at starting, but the expert and highly finished style of Pooley at the wicket tended in a great measure to change the favourable opinion formed at the outset of the encounter[119]

The *Daily Telegraph* reported that:

the wickets were not quite up to the usual Oval excellence, the parched up and thirsty ground being, like other grounds, evidently sadly in need of a long downpour of heavy wet.
"Pooley kept wicket and 'kept' so finely that he caught out five and stumped another thus taking six out of the first seven, being a wicket-keeping feat rarely surpassed in first class matches

The *Telegraph* reporter also adds that Payne was dismissed by a remarkable clever legside catch at the wicket.[120]

The following day, the same newspaper, apparently a little more records and statistics conscious than its competitor, reports that:

Lillywhite was stumped by Pooley and a splendid stump (the ball taken on the leg side) that was the best bit of wicket-keeping in this great wicket-keeping match.
Pooley's wicket-keeping was something extraordinary in its effectiveness for we doubt if ever before in an eleven a side match, the wicket-keeper had twelve of the wickets as Pooley did in this. (In 1862 on the Oval, the Hon C G Lyttelton,

[118] *S and B* Vol XII p 408
[119] *The Times* 7 July 1868
[120] *Daily Telegraph* 7 July 1868

the wicket-keeper for the Free Foresters had six wickets - three stumped and three caught - in the second innings of the Surrey Club and Ground).[121]

Bell's Life the following week-end comments on Pooley's extraordinary form and its contribution to the result, but then goes on to say that space compels the account of the match to be limited. [122]

While Pooley never again approached the dizzy heights of 12 wickets in a match, the next three were not exactly a drought: his form was such that he had eight victims in the next match and six in each of the following two. Within the space of two weeks then, he had 32 victims (16 catches and 16 stumpings) in four matches, none of which had required the third day.

Given the variations in the pace and bounce of pitches at the time, it was an extraordinary sequence and one which can rarely, if ever, have been surpassed in the history of the first-class game, either in quality of performance or in statistical terms. His dismissals are analysed in the table below.

	1st Innings		2nd Innings		
	Ct	St	Ct	St	
Sussex (Oval) 6 7 July	5	1	3	3	12
Kent (Gravesend) 9 10 July	1	2	3	2	8
Notts (Oval) 13 14 July	1	3	2	-	6
Lancs (Oval) 16 17 July	-	5	1	-	6
TOTAL	7	11	9	5	32

His performance at Gravesend was apparently no less spectacular than that at The Oval. The *Sporting Life* reported:

We regret that we have no space to give full details of this match which took place at Gravesend on Thursday and Friday. It would, however, be unfair not to take notice of the excellence of the Surrey wicket-keeper. In fact, it is not too much to say that the display of talent shown on Thursday by the Surrey wicket-keeper was equal to any ever exhibited - even to his performances on Monday

---

[121] *Daily Telegraph* 8 July 1868
[122] *Bell's Life* 11 July 1868

and Tuesday last on the Oval, when he participated in the downfall of no less than six Sussex wickets in either innings.[123]

In other matches, once again, he and Southerton were too much for Southgate.

Against Southerton, with Pooley behind the wicket, Southgate could do next to nothing on a most difficult pitch. With Pooley behind the wicket he was in a wet season a formidable bowler in the extreme[124]

As well as an outstanding wicket-keeper, Pooley had now become a hardened professional. Only one instance of 'Obstructing the Field' is recorded in first-class cricket before 1899 and he was involved in it. The occasion was the match against Cambridge University at The Oval on June 18-20 1868.

Considerable dissatisfaction was occasioned by Mr Absolom being given out at a critical point of the game for 'obstructing the field' ; the manner of which was as follows. The ball being returned to the wicket after an overthrow which supplemented a drive for 6 by Mr Absolom, struck the gentleman's bat as he was running and the umpire (Tanner) being appealed to by the Surrey wicket-keeper, and believing that the bat was purposely placed in the way of the ball, gave the striker out, in accordance with Rule 36. Mr Absolom was offered another innings which he, of course, declined.[125]

A pencilled hand-written note against a less detailed report of the incident in *Scores and Biographies* in The Oval Library states that the obstruction was completely accidental, though there is no way of ascertaining whether or not this is the unbiassed comment of an eye-witness. This was, incidentally, a match Surrey won after following on, an achievement not to be repeated until 1995

At the end of the 1868 season, another outstandingly successful one for Pooley, if not for Surrey, Edgar Willsher took a group of twelve players, Pooley among them, on a tour of the United States and Canada. A century and a bit before Concorde made it possible to have breakfast in London and four hours later repeat the exercise in New York, the project was a tribute to the adventurous spirit - or foolhardiness - of nineteenth-century professional

---

[123] *Sporting Life* 11 July 1868
[124] Bettesworth *The Walkers of Southgate* p 200-1
[125] *Cricketers Companion* p 39

cricketers. No sweethearting as an excuse this time. Quite the contrary: he had been married for five years and had two small daughters and while it would be idle guesswork to say that he welcomed the opportunity to get away, the tour fee would doubtless have been an attraction. Haygarth writes as follows:

On Wednesday September 2nd 1868 an Eleven (12 men) of England sailed from Liverpool for New York by the *City of Baltimore*, one of the Inman packets, to play a series of matches in the United States and Canada. The Eleven which (by request) had been chosen by Mr V E Walker, consisted of E Willsher (Captain), G Griffith, T Humphrey, H Jupp, E Pooley, James Lillywhite jun, H Charlwood, Joseph Rowbotham, John Smith (of Cambridge), Alfred Shaw, G Tarrant and G Freeman. R Daft, T Hayward, R Carpenter, G Wootton and G Summers were asked, but were unable to go. The Eleven arrived at New York on the 13th after a fine passage of ten days and nineteen hours. They played in six matches, winning five and one was drawn. They left New York on October 24th in the same ship that took them out, and reached Queenstown on November 2nd and the following day were landed at Liverpool. The return passage occupied but ten days.[126]

There had been a previous tour of North America in 1859, but none of the present squad had taken part in that. Most of the team were very sea-sick on the way out. Pooley shared a cabin with George Freeman, the Yorkshire fast bowler, but their cricketing talents were of little avail against a tempestuous ocean, as they began to question the wisdom of crossing the North Atlantic for half a dozen games of cricket, when there was plenty of opportunity to play at home.[127] Travelling within America too must have been particularly arduous. The six matches were compressed into a month between 16 September and 16 October, and were all against Twenty-twos, firstly the St George's Club in New York, then to Montreal for Twenty Two of Canada, back to Boston, then to Germanstown for Twenty-Two of Philadelphia, all but one native-born Americans, then Twenty-Two of the United States on the same ground and finally back to New York for Twenty-Two of that city.

Pitch preparation in Boston seems to have left something to be desired and might at another time and place have resulted in 25 points being deducted:

The ground was the most 'duffing' one ever seen. The wicket was laid with thick, coarse, grassy turf, with holes in it big enough to lose the ball. In addition, as it

---

[126] *S & B* Vol X p 645
[127] Pullin *Talks with Old English Cricketers* p 140

had rained without stopping for five days previously, the outsides were covered with water and mud. It was impossible to display the real science of the noble game under such circumstances.[128]

What should they know of England who only England know?

---

[128] *S & B* Vol X p 655

CHAPTER 5

CRIMINAL - LAMBETH POLICE COURT
(1869)

1869 saw a decline in Surrey's performances in that only three matches out of thirteen were won, but not in Pooley's own contribution with five first-class fifties, his highest batting average so far, as well as 33 catches and 24 stumpings. It also saw one of the first manifestations of those "faults of private character that marred Pooley's career"[129]

The nature of the faults is not specified in detail, but the three incidents which brought Pooley notoriety off the field at roughly four year intervals (this one and the later ones at Sheffield and Christchurch in 1873 and 1877 respectively) were associated with gambling, colourful language, aggression and a short fuse of a temper. It is not a digression from the purely cricketing aspects of Pooley's life to include them at the appropriate points for there is evidence of aggression on the field of play and, as cricket has been seen as an epitome of life, it is unreasonable to suppose that a man's characteristics and temper differ according to whether he is on or off the field.

The first recorded brush with the police came in 1869 when Pooley appeared in the Lambeth Police Court accused of assaulting a journalist. The building still exists, a date of 1869 very clearly displayed on the front, so the likelihood is that the fiery-tempered Edward was one of its first customers: it is now the Jamyang Buddhist Temple - quite a metamorphosis. It stands on Renfrew Road in Lambeth, adjacent to the Lambeth Workhouse where some three decades later, after a number of adventures, cricketing and otherwise, Pooley was to spend his last days.

The background to the incident which caused him to have a criminal record was that a journalist, E H Pickering of the *Sporting Life* had written about Pooley's performance in the Gentlemen v Players match in what Pooley considered to be derogatory terms. Roger Packham in his article in *Wisden Cricket Monthly* in October 1982, *The Troubles of Edward Pooley* suggests that the match in question was the Gentlemen of the South v Players of the South at The Oval. That appears unlikely as the facts do not fit, that match

---

[129] *Wisden* 1908 p 149

having begun on 15 July, the day *after* the court appearance and Pooley's brush with the court at worst left him unaffected and at best inspired him to participate in an opening partnership of 142 with Henry Jupp for the first wicket.

He had made a major contribution to the Gentlemen v Players match at The Oval on 24, 25 and 26 June: it had been closely contested and resulted in a narrow win for the Gentlemen by 17 runs. *Wisden* reported[130] that Pooley hit freely, finely and far. 62 were required to win in the Players' second innings when Wootton joined Pooley.

At 197 the wicket-keeper should have run out Wootton but did not, then an overthrow for 4 was (to the uproarious delight of the onlookers) backed up by a hit for four by Pooley, whereupon the score stood at 22 to win, and the time at 20 minutes to 7; then a 4 by Wootton drove the spectators half crazy with excitement, and then came "the end", Pooley being bowled (off his pad) for 52, so thus with 15 minutes of time, after three days' [sic] of hard, exciting and evenly played cricket, and out of a gross total of 915 runs, the Gentlemen won this grandly contested match by 17 only.

Not all reports were as complimentary, Pickering writing in the *Sporting Life* that Pooley's innings was devoid of that elegance of finish which characterised the batting of Summers and Silcock. Compared with what both broadsheet and tabloid journals produce today, what Pickering had written was fairly mild. Nineteenth century press reports are very detailed and place general emphasis on fact rather than opinion. Inevitably, the balance changes over time as other forms of the media (radio, television and the Internet) are first with the facts, leaving the newspapers to downsize their importance and gain their readers' attention with incisive criticism of the play and/or titillate their interest with personal matters far removed from cricket.

So, in the climate of the time, Pooley may have had some justification for feeling offended. What had less justification was his taking the law into his own hands.

Let *The Sportsman* take up the story. Under the headline " The Surrey Wicket-Keeper before the Magistrates", it reported:

---

[130]   Ib   1870 pp 71-2

Edward Pooley the well-known Surrey wicket-keeper appeared in the Lambeth Police Court before Mr Elliott to answer a summons for using threatening and disgusting language to Mr E H Pickering, a reporter of the staff of the *Sporting Life* who also required that Pooley should be bound over to keep the peace. Mr D Straight instructed by Mr H Leary appeared for the complainant and Mr Mayo for the defendant.

In opening the case Mr Straight said it was the duty of the complainant to criticise and report matches on behalf of the journal on which he was engaged. Probably the magistrate knew that Pooley was a skillful [sic] player, and no doubt from the proficiency he had shown entitled to represent his county. But unfortunately for himself he had not yet been taught that adverse criticism though unpleasant was very necessary. Young players who achieved a certain notoriety, and were puffed up a few times, seemed always to expect such treatment, or in default they felt inclined to take the law into their own hands to secure it. In the present case he would show that exception had been taken to the defendant's style and that in consequence he had behaved in a most blackguardly manner, and used filthy language. It appeared that on July 2 Mr Pickering was standing opposite the refreshment bar at the Oval when Pooley came up and asked if he reported for the *Sporting Life*. On receiving a reply in the affirmative, Pooley said 'What do you mean by writing in your newspaper that my innings in the Gentlemen v Players match was devoid of the elegance and finish that characterised the batting of Summers and Silcock?'[131]

In a scene that could almost have come from a Gilbert and Sullivan operetta, Pickering tells the court:

'He threatened to punch my head if only I would put my hands up and offered to stake a sovereign if I would fight. He also used some very disgusting language [the details are unfit for publication]. He did not seem the worse for liquor.'

Mr Straight, prosecuting, suggested Pooley had behaved in a blackguardly manner and used filthy language and Mr Mayo, defending, found the charge very trifling.

It appeared that certain reports in newspapers during the last two years had reflected badly on Pooley who, having heard that the complainant had stated that he had lost a match, asked with regard to it and said that he (Pooley) only wanted a fair chance. He lost his temper and mentioned something about a fight and 'punching' Pickering's head, but of course, he never intended to do it. Pooley, he might add, was held in the highest estimation by the Surrey club and it was by the Secretary who felt strongly on the matter that he (Mr Mayo) appeared on the defendant's behalf. He wishes to impress on the magistrate

---

[131] *Sportsman* 15 July 1869

that Pooley never intended doing Pickering any harm and considered that if he expressed a little regret and paid the costs, the complainant's counsel could have no objection.[132]

Mr Straight thought Mr Pickering should have an ample apology for an unprovoked attack and disgusting language used by Pooley. The magistrate, Mr Elliott, required a full apology to be made, bound Pooley over to keep the peace, required him to find a surety of £10 and pay the costs.

Pooley endeavoured to make a statement of what he considered his grievance, but Mr Elliott suggested that the less he said the more creditable it would be to himself and by the advice of his attorney, Pooley expressed his sorrow for having threatened to punch the defendant's head and apologised for his bad language. A surety having been found, both sides left the Court.[133]

The episode did not have any detrimental effect on his form and he continued to enjoy an outstanding season, both with the gloves and the bat and to be the hero of The Oval crowds. It is a maxim among professional cricketers that critics are best answered with bat and ball, rather than pen and tongue (or fists!) and Pooley seems to have set about doing that. His performances for the Players and the Players of the South have already been mentioned in the context of the court case, but there were some outstanding contributions to Surrey and the USEE.

At The Oval in August, Surrey replied to Middlesex's 76 with 353, thanks to some "brilliant cricket by Pooley, 88, and Jupp 106"[134] Middlesex fared rather better in the second innings, but still left Surrey just 37 to win. In a spectacular attempt to snatch defeat from the jaws of victory, they lost eight wickets in doing so to "splendid fielding and some great bowling by Howitt"[135], batsmen departing at 0, 15, three at 16, 18, 26 and 31. Throughout the mayhem, Pooley, having opened the innings, stood firm with an uncharacteristic 14 not out, concluding after the fall of the eighth wicket with a four, a single and a bye and seeing Surrey to victory.

[132] Ib
[133] Ib
[134] Bettesworth *The Walkers of Southgate* p 294
[135] *Wisden* 1870 p 81

It was in 1870 that *Wisden* in its seventh edition started reporting on matches, rather than just giving the scorecards. The comments it has on Pooley's performances vary from the complimentary -

the very "steady" cricket played by Pooley, who was about 2 hours and a half at the wicket for his 69 the steadiest "long innings" Pooley ever played [136]

to the euphoric -

Pooley's 35 was a fine sample of brilliant hitting, and six wickets told he was in form with the gloves. [137]

The "brilliant hitting" certainly seems to have been more characteristic than the "steadiness" . Against Kent at The Oval

Pooley and Mr Potter made 50 before the first Surrey wicket fell: in Pooley's 48, there was a 7 (overthrow for 4) a 5, four 4's and three 3's [138]

and in the second innings

Pooley left with the score at 20 of which *runs Pooley had made 19 in 10 minutes by a 5, a 4, three 3's and a single* [139].

For a number of years, Pooley was one of the attractions of the Canterbury Festival of which *Wisden* writes:

"The week" of all weeks in the cricketing season is this, annually held in August on the St Lawrence ground at Canterbury. As a Cricket County gathering of all classes from Peer to Peasant, it never had an equal, and as a Cricket "week" played out by the most eminent Amateurs and Professionals in the country, it is far away beyond rivalry. [140]

It goes on to refer to the fielding and comments that the wicket-keeping of Pooley and Plumb was "very fine" and gave special pleasure to the

[136]	Ib	p 78
[137]	Ib	p 67
[138]	Ib	p 82
[139]	Ib	p 83
[140]	Ib	p 52

onlookers, "but as 'the week' wore on the fielding lost character". Was it not ever thus with "weeks" and tours? In the Surrey batting averages, Pooley was second to Jupp; in all first-class cricket he scored 780 runs at an average of 21.08, 33 catches and 24 stumpings.

CHAPTER 6

THE GOLDEN YEARS
(1870/1872)

1870 was among Surrey's worst ever seasons: by the time they were defeated by Gloucestershire at The Oval in July by an innings and 129 runs, they had lost twelve consecutive county matches[141], a feat unparalleled in the Club's history. Against Sussex, after one over from Southerton, they stood at 2 for 3[142] They even contrived to lose to Middlesex whose fixture list was severely curtailed because they were at the time without a home ground. It was a match which perhaps epitomised the season of poor team performances, but outstanding individual contributions from Pooley.

In their second innings Pooley and Griffith hit the score from 25 for 3 wickets to 130 for 4; and Pooley and T Humphrey hit it from 130 for 4 to 190 for 5, when Pooley was had at short leg for 90 [sic - actually 94]. So many as 167 runs were made while Pooley was in; his hitting was brilliant. His 94 included a drive for 6 from Howitt, a 5 and six fours.[143]

It was his highest first-class score to date, one of six first-class fifties and part of 1084 first class runs that season made at an average of 23.06.

It was not until August that the tide began to turn for Surrey when they won five out of their last six fixtures to provide a veneer of respectability to the season: they turned the tables on a weakened Middlesex, Lancashire were beaten in two days by an innings and 15 runs and Kent also in two days by an innings and 43. In the process, Kent were dismissed in their first innings in 50 minutes for 20, "one of the smallest innings made by a county Eleven".[144] They have not had a smaller one since.

Throughout the season, Pooley as a batsman was at his peak and although unable to keep wicket in every match because of injuries to his hands, none the less continued to entertain and endear himself to the crowds, especially at The Oval where, despite Surrey's poor results, the crowds remained vociferous and supportive. C I Thornton recalls that:

---

[141] *S &B* Vol XI p 443
[142] *Wisden* 1871 p 75
[143] Ib   p 74
[144] *S & B* Vol XI p 488

In another match at the Oval the crowd became very angry because I bowled three of their favourites, Jupp. Humphrey and Pooley, and they began to shout 'Take the ----------- off'. Willsher, the famous old Kent bowler, then walked to the ring and said to them, 'Look here. If you can't behave yourself in a respectable way we shall not play any more. See?' They saw and became quiet[145]

We have seen in a previous chapter how Pooley's appeal resulted in C A Absolom being given out 'Obstructing the Field' in the Cambridge University fixture. He now turned his attention to the other University and was instrumental in the suspension for several years of the fixture with Oxford. While Pooley was not involved in the incidents in the sixties that had resulted in the Yorkshire and Nottinghamshire fixtures being discontinued, they had formed part of his learning curve, part of an atmosphere which he had absorbed. He had now become involved in the great nineteenth century tradition of other first-class teams refusing to play against Surrey. The incident this time was a dispute over the run out of Mr Nepean[146].

Apparently an appeal for LBW had been answered with 'not out'. Nepean failed to hear the 'not' and left the crease. Pooley broke the wicket and appealed successfully for a run out.[147] It could not happen today. Under Law 27.5 the umpires have an obligation to intervene in such circumstances. *Wisden* makes no mention of the incident, being more concerned with "20 minutes' late commencement each morning, and inexcusable waste of time at luncheons."[148]

The matter assumed a high profile. The President of MCC wrote to the President of Surrey and a special Committee meeting was called. Caesar and Mortlock, the two umpires were examined as was Pooley and the conclusion reached that there was no evidence of unfair play or intention.[149] The fixture was not renewed for over ten years.

If Pooley engaged in 'gamesmanship' he was not alone, being at the non-striking end on his way to 87 not out in the incident at The Oval three weeks

[145] W A Bettesworth *Chats on the Cricket Field* p 351
[146] *S & B* Vol XI p 379
[147] G Derek West *Twelve Days of Grace* p 94
[148] *Wisden* 1871 p 76
[149] Surrey County Cricket Club minutes 14 July 1870 Surrey County Record Office 2041/1/2

later when Southerton was famously recorded in *Scores and Biographies* as "retired, thinking he was caught 0".[150]

Scores and Biographies makes no further comment. *Wisden* embellishes slightly:

Southerton cut a ball hard on to the ground, which Mr Grace at point caught from the bound. Southerton thought the ball went straight from the bat to Mr Grace's hands, but neither of the umpires, point, nor "any other man" but Southerton thought so (Mr Grace did not toss the ball up); however, Southerton walked away and although called back, did not walk back, so he lost his innings.[151]

In a contradictory, but more colourful version, G Derek West describes the incident as follows:

Fully aware that the off-breaker shut his eyes when making a hit, the Champion indulged in a little joke which unfortunately went wrong. Throwing up the ball, he called out, "That's a hot 'un, Jim" and returned it to the bowler. To everyone's amazement, Southerton strode away....Ted Pooley, the non-striker, uttered a piercing whistle to attract his partner's attention, but W G, rather unwisely, persisted with his little joke, saying, "Keep quiet, Pooley, and we'll have the laugh at him." [152]

So, contrary to the usual pattern, Pooley and Surrey were on the wrong end of the gamesmanship on this occasion.

But, gamesmanship aside, both at The Oval and elsewhere, Pooley was appreciated by the crowds, and by none more so than the festival-goers at Canterbury. On his innings for the South against the North, *Wisden* has yet another Pooley purple passage.

For continuous big hitting and rapid scoring, Pooley's 78 on Wednesday evening topped all. It was one of those dashing onslaughts on the bowling for which the little Surrey wicket-keeper is so famous; he never hit in finer form than on that evening. He and Mr Yardley hit the score from 92 to 127 when Mr Yardley was out and Mr Thornton went in; the hitting then became marvellous in its severity. It was 5 minutes to 6 when Mr Thornton went in; in less than half an hour the score increased from 127 to 165; at 25 minutes to 7, 200 was up; at a quarter to 7, it was 225; and when at 12 to 7, Pooley was cleverly run out, the score was 230, 103 runs having been made in 53 minutes, Pooley *having in one hour and*

---

[150] *S & B* Vol XI p 435
[151] *Wisden* 1871 p 81
[152] West *Twelve Days of Grace* p 27

10 minutes made 78, including one 5 (4 for an overthrow) and fourteen 4's; his brilliant hitting evoked a succession of cheers such as are rarely heard off the Oval, and none recollected a Canterbury cricket audience as that that cheered Pooley.[153]

It was an innings that in later years Pooley himself was to recall with affection, though with an exaggeration characteristic of old men and anglers: 103 in 53 minutes becomes 130 or 140 in half an hour and the hits went higher and further than they ever did in reality.[154] The older we get, the better we were.

As well as Surrey and North v South fixtures, Pooley also made an impact in the Gentlemen of the South v Players of the South match at The Oval.

The Players' innings is noteworthy, from the fact of Pooley going in with the score at 67 for 2 wickets *and taking his bat out* for 87 (the largest innings in the match), the total 230[155]

The USEE continued to travel the length and breadth of the country. They had by now attracted W G Grace to their ranks. He was in due course to take over the side, use the professionals as his mercenaries and derive a significant amount of his income from their activities. As well as matches against Twenty-Twos, they also played some first-class cricket, including three matches against the United North of England XI, though on other occasions the cricket was obviously part of a much larger carnival. They lost by an innings and 40 runs against 18 of I Zingari on the Earl of Stamford's patch at Enville Hall, but that seems almost incidental.

About 30,000, visited the match, there being, of course, no charge.
Ethardo, the gymnast, went through his performance each day; also the Christy Minstrels, and there were many other amusements.
There was also a bazaar in connection with the cricket match, held in the conservatory, which was quite a success, the proceeds going to the restoration of the parish church.[156]

---

[153] *Wisden* 1871 p 51
[154] Pullin *Talks with Old English Cricketers* pp 135-6
[155] *Wisden* 1871 pp 80-1
[156] *S & B* Vol XI p 408

Jupp, Pooley and Humphrey maintained their unbeaten single wicket record, beating an Eleven of Middlesex (so-called) by an innings and 20 runs at Tufnell Park. *Wisden* with apparent astonishment comments:

Pooley bowled. His bowling had 5 (out of 9) in the first innings of Middlesex and *all the eleven in the second.*[157]

It was not, however, for his bowling that Pooley will be remembered in 1870. Other first class exploits apart, he topped the Surrey batting averages with just under 25 and of his 43 catches and 36 stumpings in first-class matches, 34 and 18 respectively were for Surrey, leading *Wisden* to comment admiringly:

POOLEY (whose hands were in a painfully battered state at one stage of the season) stumped 18 and caught 34 in the Surrey matches of 1870; of those 52 wickets, 13 were stumped and 18 caught from Southerton's bowling. In the Gloucestershire match on Durdham Down Pooley had 5 wickets. In one of the Middlesex matches he also had 5. In the Kent match at Mote Park, he had 6 wickets, and in the Yorkshire match on the Oval he had 7, accomplishing in that match the great wicket-keeping feat *of taking six wickets in one innings*[158].

If the team of the early seventies had, like their counterparts of 120 years later, a tune to accompany them to the wicket, it might well have been "Things can only get better." But they didn't. The following season, only one match out of seventeen was won, and that, against MCC, by the narrow margin of one wicket with five minutes to spare. Professionals past their best were retained and the need for new blood became apparent[159], but, as Ross points out in his history of the club, the barren years of the seventies were not without fine players including Jupp, one of the best defensive batsmen, Southerton, the best bowler and Pooley the greatest wicket-keeper[160]

Caffyn comments:

Gloucestershire, thanks to the three Graces, was becoming a formidable antagonist to any county who might oppose her. Surrey, though not the Surrey

---

[157] *Wisden* 1871 p 151
[158]   Ib   p 91
[159] Gordon Ross *The Surrey Story* p 31
[160]   Ib   pp 35-6

of old, possessed some of the best known names in England such as Jupp, Humphrey, Pooley and Southerton.[161]

It was against Gloucestershire, however, in early June 1871 that Pooley had one of his five fifties of the season, he and Jupp (70) added 60 in 50 minutes in a partnership which was eventually worth 89, Pooley driving W G for five and Jupp cutting him for four.[162]

He followed that a fortnight later with another half-century against Cambridge University, then at the end of the month, for the Players of the South against the Gentlemen of the South, Pooley made his only first-class century, 125, run out in the second innings, having been stumped off W G for 16 in the first. Again, Pooley shared in a rapid partnership with Jupp, this time of 121, then in a further one with Lillywhite and at the close on the second day, the Players second innings had reached 278 in 200 minutes. Pooley completed his century next morning and his innings contributed to what at the time was the highest match aggregate (1139) and to a narrow three run win by the Players, 173 and 398 against 323 and 245, Southerton taking 6 for 95 in the second innings.[163]

It was a few days later that Pooley played in Willsher's benefit match for Married v Single at Lord's, though by this time his own marriage did not have too much longer to run The fixture was a spasmodic one, having been played on only half a dozen other occasions, in 1829, 1831, 1844, 1849, 1858 and 1892.

His most memorable innings of the season, however, was once again at the Canterbury Festival. With a finger broken in a previous match and unfit to play, Pooley was only there for the beer, but found himself batting just before lunch on the first day. He recalls, more accurately than in some cases, at least as far as his own score was concerned but with characteristic exaggeration in other aspects of the story, that in the Sussex-Surrey match at Brighton, the ball had caught him on the top of the forefinger causing blood to percolate through the arm of his flannel jacket and the bone of the finger to protrude through the skin. A surgeon put the joint in splints and declared that Pooley would not be able to play cricket for months.   Shortly

---

[161] *Seventy-One Not Out* p 229
[162] Webber *Chronicle of W G* p 119
[163] *S & B* Vol XII p 129
    Webber *Chronicle of WG* p 122

afterwards, however, he played at the Canterbury Festival, having gone along as a spectator, but was dragged out of the bar to score a rapid 93. The 93 is right, the rest of the story at least questionable. [164]

Haygarth refers to "a swollen finger"[165], so perhaps Pooley may be exaggerating the incident for dramatic effect. There is plenty of evidence in contemporary accounts that his finger was injured. Against Kent a week later, for instance:

Pooley was unable to play his second innings, and after "keeping" for a few overs was compelled to give up the gloves [166]

He missed the match against Notts at Trent Bridge the following week and did not return to full wicket-keeping duties until the end of August, but as to not being able to play for several months…That interval was slightly curtailed in that he played in Surrey's very next fixture, which immediately followed the Sussex match. This was against MCC at The Oval which, as mentioned above, brought the only win of the season.

Pooley and Southerton increased the County score from 160 for 7 wickets to 335 for 8. Southerton faced Pooley at 10 minutes past 4; at 10 minutes to 5 the score was 200, at 8 minutes to 6 the score was 262, at 6.30 the 300 was up, and in the succeeding 27 minutes 35 runs were added to the score, then - when the last over of the day was being bowled - Wootton at short-leg threw out Southerton, and so, as the clock struck 7, was the 8th Surrey wicket obtained with the score at 335, thereupon the first day's play ceased - Pooley *not out* 82, Southerton *out* 82. They had been 2 hours and 50 minutes at wickets, during which bowling of every variety of pitch, pace, delivery, and style had been vainly pegging away at their wickets…….
Pooley *not out* 88, a fine hitting innings and a plucky one, inasmuch as an inflamed and swollen forefinger (put out of joint the preceding week) pained him greatly for the greater portion of the innings[167]

It was Southerton's highest first-class score.

In its report on the Canterbury match *Wisden* refers to Pooley's "battered, bruised and very painful finger", comments first on his partnership with W G Grace, then I D Walker and compares the time for his first 25 (1hr 28

---

[164] Pullin *Talks with Old English Cricketers* p 135
[165] *S & B* Vol XII p 224
[166] *Wisden* 1872 p 94
[167] *Wisden* 1872 p 93

mins) with that for the next 68 (1hr 15 mins). He added 48 for the fourth wicket with Grace and 111 for the seventh with Walker.

Pooley battled on bravely for the remainder of the season, playing in the next match against Nottinghamshire at The Oval and throughout the remainder of August but did not keep wicket. Unfit for the Gentlemen v Players match at Hove on 14, 15 and 16 August, he turned out on exactly the same dates for the USEE against Twenty-Two of Loughborough[168]. The injury was perhaps not as spectacular as made out in the Old Ebor interview, but in the next century would have been serious enough to justify a few matches rest. At the time, however, professional cricketers were remunerated on a match-by-match basis, not by the season; if they didn't play, they lost money, so they played when they were not really fit enough to do so.

Ironically, it is around this time that Haygarth draws attention to Surrey's relaxation of the previous "native born" only policy:

Some seasons back when in the height of their prosperity, Surrey strongly objected to any but "native born" appearing for or against the County. Now, however, no such objection was made by Surrey, and Martin, Gregory and Southerton, who were not born in the County, appeared regularly in the Eleven.[169]

Had it only been known that one of the County's favourite sons was by birth a Welshman!...

Although the finger injury meant that Pooley had only half as many wicket-keeping victims as he had in 1870 and for the latter part of the season had to pass the gloves to a variety of stand-in keepers (Jupp, H H Stephenson, P King and Griffith are mentioned by *Wisden*[170]) his batting did not suffer either in statistical terms (926 runs at 23.77) or in terms of public entertainment.

Pooley's 30 was one of his own special brilliant bits of batting; by his two 5's and three 4's he made 22 runs in 5 hits[171]

---

[168] *S & B* Vol XII pp 239/40
[169]   Ib   p 231
[170] *Wisden* 1872 p 103
[171]   Ib   p 24

Pooley's 51 was a fine, free dashing bit of hitting that included three 5's [172]

His 52 against Notts in the return match at The Oval comprised a six, a five and four fours. [173]

And on his hundred

From thence, Jupp and Pooley so rapidly piled up the runs that by 5 minutes after 6 the 200 was up....Jupp was first man in at 25 minutes to 4 and fourth out at 20 past 6 with the score at 224. In the succeeding 40 minutes Pooley and Lillywhite added 54 runs to the score, as when play ceased at 7 o'clock the Players' second innings shaped as follows:-
4 wickets down; 278 runs scored. Pooley not out 93, Lillywhite not out 18
On Saturday the pavilion seats were crammed, and the ground thronged by about 7000 of the most excitable visitors that ever congregated on the Oval; and from 7 minutes to 12 when play was renewed, until 10 minutes to 7, when this wonderful match was finished by Southerton, an especially strong dose of exciting cricket was played. [174]

And so to 1872 - and there were several off the field changes at The Oval, most importantly the appointment of a paid Secretary, C W Alcock who was to dominate the administration, pioneer the F A Cup and have an influence on cricket in particular and sports administration in general that spread far beyond the confines of Kennington.

Talent money arrangements were modified and a hundred years ahead of their time, Surrey tried to purchase players on a then non-existent transfer market.

This season the Surrey Club for the first time attempted (but failed) to engage cricketers of note from other counties as club bowlers for the season. Luckily, perhaps, for the credit of the county, none could be obtained; for though their pay would have been good, they could not have played in county matches for some time at least. Subsequently Surrey did obtain several foreigners and mercenaries, but their introduction has been hugely disapproved of in the "cricketing world". [175]

---

[172]   Ib   p 84
[173]   Ib   p 98
[174]   Ib   p 87
[175]   S & B Vol XII P 383

Turnstiles were erected at the old entrance and plans introduced for the tavern to be pulled down and rebuilt; a small committee room was added to the racquet end of the pavilion.

On the field too, things began to look up. For the first time since 1865, more matches were won than lost. The *Sporting Life* observed

Under the vigorous researches of the fresh Secretary Mr C W Alcock, a wonderful number of new and rising cricketers have been unearthed from the various clubs and villages to the Surrey side of the metropolis. [176]

In his rallying cry to the AGM on 2 May 1872, Alcock had set the scene:

...it was now the fashion to decry Surrey and Surrey cricket, not only by the enemies of the county, but he feared by many of its well wishers, whose allegiance a series of unforeseen defeats had somewhat shaken.....
With the names of Jupp, Pooley and R Humphrey they need not despair; they had the best wicket-keeper in the world and the best bowler in the south of England. [177]

The season's campaign started well: MCC were dismissed for 16, the lowest total against Surrey. The injuries of the previous season now behind him, Pooley's wicket-keeping was again back on song. He had 28 catches and 31 stumpings, 20 and 18 for Surrey, almost half of them in combination with Southerton. The old confidence and elegance were back.

Pooley took the ball leg side and swept down the wicket with one action [178]

and although, in terms of aggregate and average, 1872 was less successful than the previous two seasons. the old belligerence and flamboyance had not left him.

Pooley then hit so freely that *his first 24 runs were made in 17 minutes...* [179]
Pooley scored all the runs made after Jupp was out ....
Pooley then hit like a horse kicking [180]

But the storm clouds were gathering - literally. At Trent Bridge

---

[176] 1 January 1873
[177] *Wisden* 1873 p 122
[178]   Ib   p 143
[179]   Ib   p 132
[180]   Ib   p 139

"The light was bad and grew gradually worse, a storm evidently brewing all round, but they played on until the score reached 180 runs; then (3.30) play was stopped by one of the most terrific outbursts of lightning, thunder, hail, rain and wind witnessed for many years in the Midlands. One account stated "In two minutes after the storm commenced every tent but the Printers' was blown down, the water lay in pools all over the ground, the flag pole was broken in twain, and many trees were dismantled." Another account recorded:- "That four tents were blown down, the trees struck with lightning, and a greater proportion of the ground submerged in water..The storm was truly alarming and will make this match a remarkable event in cricket annals."

A third local account thought it:-"The most violent storm ever witnessed in the district. To say it rained would be ridiculous; it poured down in torrents, and not only flooded the ground, but, with the assistance of the wind and lightning, tore down the refreshment and the ladies' booths as though they were mere shreds of paper."[181]

Finally, more controversy. There is but a handful of *Unusual Dismissals* in the nineteenth century recorded in *Wisden* - and Pooley was involved in two of them. We've had the 'Obstructing the Field'; now it's 'Hit the Ball Twice'. The scene is the 'New County Ground' at Brighton; the scoreline: Charlwood..hit the ball twice..73.

The match looked well for Sussex and better still when Reed and Charlwood had increased the score to 151, but then an infringement of Rule XX lost Charlwood his wicket and, in all probability Sussex the match. Charlwood played the ball, but seeing it rolling towards the wicket, hit it hard, he at the time being over the crease and his partner, Reed, half way down the wickets backing up for the run. Pooley appealed to Caesar, the umpire, at the batsman's end, and Caesar gave Charlwood out for violating Rule XX. This caused much unpleasant excitement, but Charlwood had to leave for a very finely played innings of 73 runs[182].

Storms and controversy of a different kind were to hit Surrey and Pooley in 1873.

---

[181]   Ib   p 150
[182]   Ib   p 177

CHAPTER 7

THE SHEFFIELD INCIDENT AND ITS AFTERMATH (1873/76)

1873 got away to a slow start: in six matches and twelve completed first-class innings, Pooley failed to top 100 runs in aggregate and managed only eight catches and seven stumpings, way below his usual rate. Then after the match on 16 and 17 June, at Bramall Lane, Sheffield, when Surrey lost by eight wickets to Yorkshire in well under two days, Pooley was summarily dismissed. Why? The reasons are not exactly crystal clear.

The Committee minutes refer to "insubordination and misconduct"[183], *Wisden* to a "deplorable occurrence"[184], *Scores and Biographies* to an "unfortunate dispute" and reports that

E Pooley's name will not be found any more in the Surrey Eleven this season. Soon after this match, at a meeting held at The Oval, it was proposed, recorded and carried unanimously that - "Pooley be suspended from playing with the United South of England Eleven until he is re-instated in the Surrey Eleven"[185]

and on the team selection for the next match against Lancashire:

Pooley did not play for Surrey having just been "turned out of the eleven"[186]
For *Lillywhite's Cricketers' Companion*

..the county have lost Pooley under circumstances that everyone must regret It may be mentioned, as a matter of history, that Pooley made his last appearance for the county on this occasion[187]

There is, however, no change to his details in the *Professionals of England* section.

Lillywhite's Cricketers' Annual under *Cricket in 1873 by Incog* says
Nothing need be said here of the events that transpired to necessitate the dismissal of Pooley from the Eleven; but the facts remain the same, that Surrey,

---

[183] SCCC mins 12 November 1873 SCRO 2042/1/3
[184] *Wisden* 1874 p 140
[185] *S & B* Vol XII p 726
[186] Ib p 735
[187] 1874 edition pp 69/70

dispirited by frequent defeats, was not at all stimulated by the further misfortune that came to it in the loss of the first wicket-keeper in the kingdom, as well as a batsman of resolute character[188] .

Contemporary press reports are scarcely more enlightening, hardly surprising perhaps, given that journalists saw their job as reporting and commenting on what happens on the field of play. The 'investigative journalism' seeking to explore whatever shady dealings might have gone on behind the scenes was not yet at the conception stage.

The *Sporting Life* simply comments that Pooley played with his usual freedom[189] and praises the quality of the catch which dismissed him. *Bell's Life* in its match report mentions that Bristow kept wicket after dinner, Pooley being absent and in its summary of the week the following Saturday[190] says to conclude its report:

Nothing else occurred to call for any special remark, if we may except the substitution of Bristoe behind the stumps for Pooley after luncheon and the refusal of the Surrey wicket-keeper to take another place in the field, consequently, the Yorkshiremen lent Clayton to the Transpontine county. Surrey, minus Pooley, then travelled to Manchester.

Do Pooley's own recollections in the 'Old Ebor' interview throw any light on the matter? Pullin refers to a "certain unpleasantness" and allegations of gambling. The "facts", as given by Pooley, are that he backed himself and Henry Jupp to score more runs than the Yorkshire pair, Andrew Greenwood and 'old Mary' Lockwood. Pooley scored the most runs and the two bottles of champagne were had for breakfast. The matter was exaggerated and it was rumoured that Pooley had sold the match for £50. Unjustifiably victimised, he was suspended for the remainder of the season. "I was never a gambler on cricket," he claims indignantly.[191]

While the bottle of champagne may perhaps explain the need to replace Pooley as wicket-keeper and his later statement that he was feeling unwell and out of sorts on the second day, "I was never a gambler on cricket" may be taken with a larger pinch of salt than even the five years knocked off his age, 140 runs in half an hour and the bone protruding through the skin. He

---

[188]   1874 edition   p 29
[189]   18 June 1873
[190]   21 June 1873
[191]   Pullin *Talks with Old English Cricketers* pp 136-7

may have forgotten - or chosen not to remember - that it was his penchant for gambling that caused him to miss out on a couple of Test Match appearances. As for the bet: if it was as he states, then there is no kind of creative accounting that would result in a win for Jupp and Pooley who made 12 & 1 and 10 & 0 respectively, while Greenwood and Lockwood made 22 & 5 and 7 & 30 not out.

For a likelier version of what happened we need to look at the letter appealing for reinstatement sent to the Committee by Pooley at the end of the season.

Oct 16 1873

To the Committee of the Surrey Club
  Gentlemen
  Now that the season is over I beg to make a statement respecting the match at Sheffield. I understand that I am charged with three things namely.
    1st That I did not try to win the match
    2nd That I did so because I had bets against my side
    Third That I used abusive language to the Captain
As regards the first of these charges, I do assure you that if I did not appear to be trying it was owing to my being unwell on the morning of the second innings and being thoroughly out of sorts and I most positively deny the fact of my intentionally giving any advantage to the other side.

As regards the bet, I took one bet of five shillings to half a crown that five Yorkshire players did not get seventy runs. I backed Mr Boult against Hall and myself against the same player for half a crown; R Humphrey and Jupp against Lockwood and Emmett for the same amount and T Humphrey against A Hill, so according to my bets the imputation is that I sold the match for half a crown.

Again as regards the first charge I plead my full career of this last thirteen years, and if at any time I have failed to give satisfaction as alleged against me I can only assure you that I have never done so from any dishonest motive but from being like other men who carry on from day to day a very arduous work get weak and tired.

As regards the third charge of using coarse language I of course plead guilty and most sincerely apologise to the Club and to those to whom I used it either at Sheffield or any other time or place.

I now ask the Committee to consider what my position has been and what it is now.

I suppose that I have been acknowledged as the best wicket-keeper in the south of England judging from the fact that I have been selected to take part in the Players v Gentlemen in London.

At my present age I have plenty of cricket left in me and I ask you now gentlemen if you will kindly reconsider a judgement that takes the bread out of my mouth and family, as a cricketer or in any other career. It is impossible for me to enter any new business with confidence or credit with a cloud hanging over me as dishonesty and errors in tempers are two different things

I hope you will do me the favor [sic] to summon me before the Committee and let me confirm what I have said in this letter.

Hoping you will look on this favourably

I am Gentlemen   Yours obt
(sgd)   E Pooley

If the bets were as Pooley stated and on the first innings, then he would have won four out of the five of them, one being void as Boult and Hall each scored two. Had they applied to the second innings as well, he would not have done quite so well, but would have been in pocket. So, if we put Pooley's two versions of the story together, the probability is that the bets were on the first innings, that Pooley won, that a bottle of champagne was involved on the second morning which was not unconnected with his being abusive to the captain and not taking the field after lunch. There appears to be no firm evidence of a bet of £50 against Surrey winning the match. As already mentioned, the minutes of the meeting refer simply to "insubordination and misconduct"[192]

The appeal was supported by Pooley's team-mates in the following terms:

We the undersigned being six of the players of the current Surrey Eleven who have played most with Pooley, having heard that he is about to apply to the Committee for restitution to the Eleven respectfully state to the Committee that we should be happy to play with him again and believe that he would do his duty to the satisfaction of the Gentlemen of the County and the Public.
(sgd) J Southerton   Henry Jupp   R Humphrey
        T Humphrey   James Street   John Bristow

In an article in *Wisden Cricket Monthly* in October 1982[193], Roger Packham says that the Committee passed a resolution to reinstate him. That is not

---

[192] SCCC mins 12 November 1873 SCRO 2042/1/3
[193] pp 40-1

strictly true. They allowed him to sweat for another three months and then summoned him before the Committee. There was a proposal at the November meeting:

That Pooley having been suspended on the report of the Match Committee during the season of 1873 for insubordination and misconduct at Sheffield and the Surrey players having interceded with the Committee of the Surrey Club on his behalf it is the opinion of this Committee that he has been sufficiently punished and that he shall be reinstated in the County Eleven in accordance with the wish of the players who have served their County truly for many years.

After discussion, that proposal was withdrawn and the Committee passed to the next business of making a donation of five guineas to the Kennington Soup Kitchen. It was only in February 1874 that Pooley, having been summoned before the Committee and apologised for his behaviour, was formally reinstated.[194]

So what happened to Pooley during his period of suspension? He refers emotively in his letter to a decision which takes the bread out of his mouth and that of his family, but the extent of the support and of the family is unclear. Daughters Ellen and Fanny were nine and eight years old respectively and it is possible that he was supporting his mother and sisters. It was, however, about this time that he began his relationship with his common law wife for the next twenty years, Minnie Sabine, then aged eighteen or nineteen and some twelve years his junior. His wife Ellen was heading towards her mid-thirties. His mistress's full name was Minnie Mary Sabine, though the 'Mary' was used only intermittently on the children's birth-certificates. There is an internet reference to a Minnie Sabine who was a 19th century pin-up girl, and while there is no firm evidence that this is the same person, second-hand family recollections that even in her later years Minnie was a very attractive woman suggest at least a likelihood. His eldest son, also named Edward, was born in 1874 and was the first of eight illegitimate children, in addition to Ellen and Fanny. Pooley's association with Minnie presumably meant the *de facto* end of his marriage to Ellen, though whether it was the cause or one of the effects it is not possible to say, nor is it possible to deduce whether Edward left Ellen or vice versa. Unusually the children stayed with the husband. It is, however, as certain as it can be that they were not divorced, as divorce was not the option it has subsequently become. It was only since 1858 that it had been

---

[194] SCCC mins 9 February 1874 SCRO 2042/1/3

possible to procure an absolute divorce through the law courts. Prior to that a special act of Parliament had been required.

Edward Albert Thomas is registered in his unmarried mother's surname of Sabine and his birth certificate has no entry in the spaces for name, surname and occupation of father. The Births and Deaths Registration Act of 1874, the year of his birth, as well as transferring the onus of registration from the Registrar to the parents, tightened the registration of illegitimate births by permitting the insertion of the father's name only when both parents attended to register the birth.[195] In this instance, it is apparent that only one did and the same applies in the case of the next three illegitimate children, Alice, John and Walter born in 1877, 1880 and 1882.

In cricket terms, Pooley continued to play for the USEE until the suspension was applied in that area too. Indeed, a couple of days after the Sheffield incident, as Surrey were appearing against Lancashire at Old Trafford, not far away at Broughton, Pooley was taking the field with the USEE against Eighteen of the Manchester Broughton Club. He continued to play for the USEE at Bradford, Leicester and Wakefield where he made his final appearance on 12 July after which his name disappears from the records. He did not feature in the Gentlemen v Players or North v South matches and for the first time for several years he was absent from the Canterbury Festival. Then, unexpectedly, there was one isolated sighting. On 25 August at Scarborough against eighteen of that Town, he turned out for the United *North* of England XI: he did not, however, usurp the regular wicket-keeper, Thomas Plumb. As one sporting newspaper wrote: "What right Pooley had to play as a member of the UNEE is not clear."[196]

However, Pooley was street-wise enough to have contingency plans against the possible failure of his appeal for reinstatement and he had taken on a beer house in Richmond, the 'Albany' in Kew Foot Road,[197] on the fringe of Old Deer Park and now separated from the town by a dual-carriageway Even by the turn of the century, it had long ceased to be a public house and had been taken over by Mr Wimple, an upholsterer and Mr Clark, a furniture dealer, who used the old skittle alley.[198] At this time, *Lillywhite's*

---

[195] Nissel *People Count* p26
[196] *S & B* Vol XII p 930
[197] *Cricketers' Companion* 1873 p 196
[198] *Licensing World* 27 July 1907

Cricketers' Companion gave the addresses of cricketers where known. Pooley remained in Richmond until 1876 and then upon his return from Australia and New Zealand until his retirement in 1883, his address was given simply as 'Kennington Oval SE'. He presumably had a *poste restante* arrangement at the ground, as he appears on the 1881 Census among the residents of Battersea, rather than those of Kennington Oval.

Meanwhile, during Pooley's suspension, cricketing matters had not gone well at The Oval. The 1872 season had proved something of a false dawn for Surrey: the following year they won three and lost ten of their fifteen first-class matches.

That Surrey suffered in wicket-keeping after the Sheffield match none can deny, for Mr Morris decidedly failed with the county gloves, and Jupp, although fairly good, is much below Pooley form at wicket-keeping[199]

It is perhaps ironic that Pooley was at his best when Surrey were at their worst and though, after his reinstatement, his wicket-keeping was as sharp and keen as ever, his batting, the style of which depended very much on flair and 'eye', never again reached the same heights. Of the 32 first-class fifties in his career, only five were made after his reinstatement, two of them in the first year of it, including 97 against Cambridge University, his highest first-class innings for Surrey. His only mention in *Wisden*'s summary of Surrey's 1874 season is bracketed with several others and is to the effect that he improved on his batting average of the previous season.[200] As that had been 8, it was hardly an earth-shattering achievement.

He had eased his way back into the game with an appearance as a "given man" for Fifteen Surrey Colts against the Surrey Club, scoring 17 and 35 and making a stumping.[201] The gods may have disapproved of his reinstatement. Hail, rain, thunder and lightning characterised the first day; then he appeared in the North v South fixture at Lord's on Whit Monday and Tuesday and top-scored with 19 not out in the South's first innings of 70. Storms had made the ground heavy and the North mustered 41 and 78. The South won by eight wickets.

---

[199] *Wisden* 1874 p 102
[200] Ib 1875 p 124
[201] *S & B* Vol XIII p 26

Surrey, however, were now increasing in strength to the extent that they declined to play Kent in 1874 and 1875. Haygarth disapproved.

This match was last played Aug 18th 1873 and it is believed that Surrey refused to play Kent in 1874 and 75 in consequence of the supposed or real inferiority of the Kent Eleven of that date. But county matches which have been played for years (and there is no older match than that between Kent and Surrey) ought not to be put on one side merely because one eleven or other is supposed to be of an inferior calibre. Eton and Harrow may as well temporarily abandon their meeting for a like cause [202]

A reference in *Wisden*'s report on the North v South match of 1875[203] to "an innings that testifies to the old Pooley form being still in full vigour" damns with faint praise, but reports on his wicket-keeping remain complimentary. Against Gloucestershire at The Oval:

Pooley thereby commenced a display of wicket-keeping really [sic] equalled and which won the match hand over hand for Surrey.
At 37 Pooley stumped Mr Miles.
Mr W Grace also "played" the bowling superbly, but in vain, as after playing three-quarters of an hour for 18 runs, "How's that?' roared Pooley, and a Surrey shout of the old intensity told the great bat was done for.
Pooley's great wicket-keeping calling to mind his wonderful display on the Oval in 1868...splendidly the little wicket-keeper merited their vociferous cheers by the grand form in which he, on the second day, pulled off the match for his County.[204]

He was still accepting engagements as a "given man", turning out in a one day match for "Sixteen Players of Richmond and District with E Pooley and R Humphrey" against the Richmond Club with W G Grace. He was c Jupp b Grace for 76 in a total of 391. It was spectator entertainment rather than a competitive occasion. The Richmond Club replied with 11 for 3 and the match was unfinished.

A "given man" is defined in Michael Rundell's *Dictionary of Cricket* as a player who is not a regular member of a team but is allowed to play for it in a particular match, often being supplied by the opposing side in an attempt

---

[202] Ib   p 1025
[203] *Wisden* 1876 p 128
[204]   p 135

to produce a more even contest.[205] What Rundell does not say is that they did not do it for free!

It was the following year, 1876, that Pooley's younger brother, Frederick, made a fleeting appearance on the first-class scene, having met with some success at Lord's for Twelve Colts of the Rest of England against Twelve Colts of Notts and Yorkshire. *Wisden* refers to "the young Pooley (who hit hard and well)" and goes on to say that

the cricket of the "Rest of England" does not require notice beyond recording F Pooley's wicket-keeping was the best shown in the match. [206]

He played for Surrey against Yorkshire at Bramall Lane, caught three, but made a pair. Big brother Ted did much better, making 0 and 1[207]. Fred also played for the USEE and was run out for 4 at no 10 against Twenty Two of Grimsby, but it hardly precipitated a crisis. At the other end W G Grace was on his way to 400 not out in a total of 681. In a real thriller, Grimsby replied with 88 for 11.[208] Haygarth points out that "F Pooley is brother to the 'crack' E Pooley. His name will be found but seldom."

Haygarth continues his lack of enthusiasm. Against MCC at Lord's, Pooley senior's four catches and as many stumpings in the match attract the comment "nearly all, however, off slow balls."[209] The twentieth century view would be that "keeping" to slow bowlers is the more skilled operation, but the comment has to be seen in the context of Pooley - and wicket-keepers generally - standing up to everything and using a long-stop for the quicker bowlers.

Of the county too, Haygarth is critical, particularly of their arranging a fixture during the Canterbury Festival:

It was not considered correct or cricket like that the Surrey Club should arrange a grand match on the same days as the "Canterbury week" inasmuch, as, thereby, no Sussex or Surrey men could assist at that festival. The Canterbury festival

---

[205] Rundell *Dictionary of Cricket* pp 97-8
[206]   1877 p 39
[207] *S & B* Vol XIII p 904
[208] *S & B* Vol XIII p 970
[209]   Ib   p 966

dates back as far as 1842, and other days could easily have been found for the above contest [210]

The alternative view is that Surrey were through their rough period of the early 70s, that their approach was now more professional and that in dropping the Kent fixture from their list and eschewing the Canterbury festival, they were seeking to improve the quality of their cricket and Pooley, having been a Surrey stalwart in those wilderness years, on return from his suspension, was as wicket-keeper, a pivotal part of that revival, even though his batting contribution might have been less than it was a few years earlier.

Not that Surrey had cause for complacency. There were still hiccups, as against Cambridge University, when

A frightful fiasco then occurred. At 6.30 Surrey's second innings was commenced; *at 7 o'clock 10 overs had been bowled, and 5 Surrey wickets were down for 7 runs.* Those wickets fell as follows:-
1/0 2/1 3 and 4/4 5/7.
The first ball delivered got Humphrey c and b; the fourth ball got Jupp caught at point; from the fourteenth ball Pooley was had at point; from the seventeenth Mr Shuter was c and b; and from the fortieth Mr Bridges was c and b. Then that astonishing evening's cricket ended, the five wickets having fallen to the following ten overs:-
MR PATTERSON W . I W . 1 . . W . . . . . 1 . . 1 . .
MR LUDDINGTON 2 . . . . W . . . 1 . . . . W   211

Pooley's popularity at The Oval was by no means diminished. In Tom Humphrey's benefit match, North v South

Mr W Grace then had Pooley facing him, and the latter roused the spectators from quietude to cheering by a spanking drive for 5; but at 120 Hill threw out Pooley, a portion of the British Public then on the Oval loudly and angrily expressing their opinion that Pooley was "not out"....they left at lunch the score at 130 for 8 wickets, Mr W Grace *not out* 47 and the B.P. in an exceedingly excited state anent Pooley's being run out.[212]

It was not his only misjudgment. Against Yorkshire

[210]   Ib   p 1067
[211] *Wisden* 1877 p 151 (The four-ball over was in use throughout most of the nineteenth century)
[212]   Ib   p 153

Pooley joined Mr Read but the new comer's stay was brief as the batsmen got in two minds about an impossible run, and the professional was the sufferer.[213]

His highest score that season was 63 against Gloucestershire at The Oval, one he was not to exceed in the remainder of his career.

the interest of the visitors had been monopolised by Pooley whose two clipping 5's (cut and leg-hit) five 4's and six 3's was quite of the old Pooley form and elicited the old form of Surrey shouts. Pooley went to the wickets with the score 32; he left with it at 129, so while he was at work, the runs made for Surrey were 97 of which he (brilliantly) made 63. [214]

Wisden was happy with his wicket-keeping performance over the season.

POOLEY was all right with the gloves; he "kept" in 14 matches for Surrey, capturing 39 wickets - 18 stumped and 21 caught out; his 4 stumped, and 4 caught in the MCC match , being quite up to the best Pooley form. [215]

His performances continued to be "all right" too for the United South, though the performances of W G continued to dominate. Against the United North at Hull, Grace made 126 out of 159; the highest proportion of a first-class total (79.2%) by an Englishman and the world record until 1943-4[216]. Pooley's 14 was the next highest score, then came 'Extras' with five. Despite a general decline in his batting ability, he had maintained a high standard of wicket-keeping and his form since reinstatement had certainly been good enough for him to be invited to be part of Lillywhite's party to tour Australia and New Zealand in the winter of 1876/77.

[213] *Bell's Life* 26 August 1876
[214] *Wisden* 1877 p 149
[215]   Ib   p 146
[216] Bill Frindall in Rae *W G: A Life* p 498

CHAPTER 8

IN COURT AGAIN - AUSTRALIA, NEW ZEALAND AND THE CHRISTCHURCH INCIDENT (1876/77)

There is no doubt whatever that, but for a certain fracas across the Tasman Sea, Edward Pooley would have been among the twenty-two immortals who took part in the first Test Match of all time on the Melbourne Cricket Ground from 15 to 19 March 1877. In the popular folklore of nineteenth century 'firsts' it ranks with Stephenson's Rocket and the Penny Black, although none of the twenty-two were aware they were playing in the inaugural Anglo-Australian Test Match. They thought they were playing in a fixture arranged between a Combined Melbourne and Sydney XI and James Lillywhite's professional touring team. Only subsequently was it deemed to be a 'Test Match'. Australia won by 45 runs, a result replicated in the Centenary Test in 1977.

That, however, was as remote in time, as Edward Pooley was remote in distance, more than 1,000 miles away, remanded on bail in Dunedin for assault and damaging property. Certainly, he would have kept in Melbourne. His understudy, Henry Jupp, played, but was too unwell to keep wicket. Selby stood in and Jupp took over in the second 'Test' two weeks later. He had been ill most of the tour, but had to play. When a touring party of twelve is reduced by one, selection problems are minimised, not to say eliminated! "Pooley," reports Haygarth, "was unable to appear for England, a great loss to his side, as the absence of Jupp had been previously".[217] Jupp's absence had been easily explicable. The reasons behind Pooley's non-appearance were more complex and more controversial.

The 'Tests' came at the end of a long and arduous tour.

The defeat of England must candidly be attributed to fatigue, owing principally to the distances they had to travel to each match, to sickness, and to high living. England never were fresh in any of their engagements and, of course, had not near their best Eleven.[218]

---

[217] *S & B* Vol XIV p 21
[218] Ib

It was almost six months earlier that the party had had a warm-up match against Twenty-two of Priory Park, Chichester just before leaving England in late September. They played their first match, in Adelaide, on November 16. Unlike previous touring parties, it was an all-professional side.

Lillywhite's men, who were representing English cricket in Australia during the season 1876-77 were all professionals. Hence it cannot be said that they stood for the full strength of England, since the amateur element was very conspicuous in our cricket about this time; but they were at least adequately representative of the players, Ephraim Lockwood being almost the only prominent professional absent. [219]

Only one first-class match was played on the first leg of the tour and that was an impromptu affair, being "got up" at the conclusion of the 'Fifteen of New South Wales' match on the Albert Ground, Sydney, "the Committee of New South Wales being ambitious to try their strength 'man for man'."[220] It was the first even-handed contest played between an England and Australian Eleven and, in his one first-class match overseas, Pooley made 36 and had one stumping.

In between, they had played against Fifteens and Twenty-twos in Sydney, Newcastle, Gouldbourn, Melbourne, Ballarat and Geelong. So, if modern touring sides sometimes complain about unreasonable travelling requirements and time spent in airport departure lounges, let them consider the preceding itinerary and then the subsequent one from Sydney to Auckland.

On January 17 1877 the England Eleven left Sydney in the SS Tararna for New Zealand (1100 miles) and on the 22nd reached Hokitika, which they left the same day and arrived at Greymouth (20 miles further) in two hours more. They then proceeded 200 more miles to Nelson. Leaving Nelson on the 25th, in the SS Wellington, they reached Taranaki on the 26th, and on the 27th arrived at Manulau harbour, and landed at Onehanga, proceeding overland to Auckland.[221]

From 29 January, they played a four day match against Twenty-two of Auckland.

[219] J N Pentelow *England v Australia 1877 to 1904* p 13
[220] *S & B* Vol XIV p 8
[221] Ib p 10

According to Southerton, who kept a diary on the tour, Lillywhite agreed he would pay an allowance of 4/- per day for drinks to each member of the team. All except one - guess who? - were happy with this. Pooley felt the offer was not sufficiently generous. Southerton observed that Pooley's "inside must be lined with some imperishable material".[222]

In New Zealand the itinerary was no less arduous : after Auckland, it was Wellington, New Plymouth, Nelson, Greymouth, Christchurch, Dunedin and finally Invercargill. Crowds were large and enthusiastic, the *New Zealand Herald and Daily Southern Cross* reporting a total attendance of some 25,000 at the match against Eighteen of Canterbury at Christchurch.[223] Pooley's jaunty and flamboyant batting style was as effective as it had been in the northern hemisphere. Against Twenty-two of Nelson, for instance,

7-236. Pooley then took the bat and with Greenwood kept the field alive for some time. [224]

Off the field, the Englishmen clearly enjoyed themselves: New Zealand cricket historian T W Reese refers to Pooley as a champion wicket-keeper, and on the rest of the team and its activities, says:

Off the ground the Englishmen had a tremendous time, and many a story is retailed of their hearty good humour and practical joking proclivities as well as some questionable practices of the team. "Happy Jack" Ulyett and "Owd" Tom Emmett were each still at the beginning of a long career, and were cheery players of the best kind of cricket. Emmett was a genuine wit and a bit of a jester in his way. Selby was a great runner and prepared to make a match at any time, and in nearly every town a running contest was part of the programme[225]

Certainly the tourists appear to have had an enjoyable time and appreciated the scenic beauty of New Zealand. Captain James Lillywhite, reporting on the tour in *Lillywhite's Cricketers' Companion* writes:

From Greymouth, we journeyed overland to Christchurch, and I recommend all travellers who can stand a good shaking to take this trip; the scenery is magnificent the whole of the distance till you get on the eastern side of the island to the Canterbury Plain. The splendid tree-ferns growing in the demi forests

[222] West *Twelve Days of Grace* p 98
[223] 1 March 1877
[224] *Otago Daily Times* 16 February 1877
[225] T W Reese *New Zealand Cricket 1841-1914* p 77

many feet high, the snow-topped mountains, the fearful gorges, winding rivers and blue lakes, all combine to make an ever changing panorama of views, said to be unsurpassed in any equal distance of coach-road in the world.
Through being stopped at the Otira Gorge by a flood, we did not arrive in Christchurch till the morning of the match, February 26th.
Upwards of 25,000 persons were on the ground during the three days, but, it being a public ground, the Eleven got very little benefit out of it thousands refusing to give anything.[226]

The *Otago Daily Times* was equally critical of the freeloaders

...as many as 10,000 must have been on the ground during the afternoon though it is lamentable to observe that a large percentage had the meanness to pass through the gates without paying their entrance fee, though of course it was entirely optional.[227]

but equally sympathetic to the travelling difficulties experienced by their guests.

The long looked-for match of the All England v Eighteen of Canterbury commenced this morning. Cricketers were on the "Qui vive" on Saturday for the arrival of the Englishmen overland from Hokitika, but the state of the rivers delayed them at Bealey, where they stopped for a night in great misery. They arrived at Malvern on Sunday afternoon and came from thence by train this morning. It may thus be presumed that the Eleven were not in first rate trim for the labours of the day[228]

Interestingly, notwithstanding the botanical and geographical descriptions of New Zealand, Lillywhite makes no mention of the Christchurch incident, except to say in his Test Match report that in the absence of Pooley, Selby kept wicket.

So what caused Pooley to be absent? Unsurprisingly, his gambling habit was at the root of his adventures. He had been ill for the match against Twenty-two of Westland at Greymouth on 20-22 February and didn't play at Christchurch against Eighteen of Canterbury. He did, however, stand as umpire, and notwithstanding a long-standing and quite understandable prohibition in the Laws of Cricket (Law XLII at the time) on umpires gambling on a match in which they were involved, struck a 20-1 bet in

---

226 *Cricketer's Companion* 34th Edition p 43
227 27 February 1877
228 Ib

shillings with one Ralph Donkin, that he would correctly forecast the first-innings score of each of the Canterbury players. He forecast a duck for each. Four out of the eighteen "failed to trouble the scorers". They also failed to trouble the umpires, all four being bowled, so it appears that Pooley was not involved in any decisions which could have been to his financial advantage. Notwithstanding that, the outcome was that Pooley had won £4 and lost 14/-, a net profit of £3/6/-. Or so he thought. Donkin claimed it was "a catch bet" and declined to pay. Trouble ensued.

The team moved on to Dunedin to play Eighteen of Otago. Fully recovered from his illness, Pooley played, had a catch and two stumpings. The spectators were impressed, the *Otago Witness* recording that "Much amusement was caused by Pooley's dexterity as wicket-keeper." and summarised his contribution to the tour in the following terms:

Pooley, the finest wicket-keeper of the day; very quick and neat in style; smart at taking leg-balls; a fine batsman[229]

It was, however, to be his last recorded appearance on a cricket ground before July. At the end of the match, "the Englishmen left by special train for Southland. They travel all night and play at Invercargill tomorrow".[230] It was an ordeal from which Pooley and the baggage man, Albert Bramall were spared. An alternative one took precedence. They were arrested. In contemporary press accounts, "Bramall" is spelled "Bramhall" and he is referred to as the money taker.

The *Otago Daily Times* reported as follows[231]

Immediately after the cricket match yesterday, Edward Pooley, the celebrated wicket-keeper, and Albert Bramhall, the money-taker for the All-England Eleven were charged with having, at Christchurch, maliciously injured the property of one Ralph Donkin, above the value of £5 and contrary to the provisions of the Malicious Injuries to Property Act. The defendants were remanded to appear at Christchurch on the 12th March current. They are admitted to bail - themselves in £100, and two sureties of £50 each.

And a week later [232]

[229] 10 March 1877
[230] *New Zealand Herald and Daily Southern Cross* 6 March 1877
[231] 6 March 1877
[232] 13 March 1877

Christchurch March 12th

At the Resident Magistrate's Court today Edward Pooley, one of the English cricketers, was charged with assaulting Ralph Donkin. Prior to the cricket match here, Donkin made a bet with Pooley, but afterwards, considering it a catch bet, sent a message to Pooley that he cried off. After the match, Pooley claimed the amount of the bet - £3/6/-. Donkin refused to pay. Pooley then assaulted him. The parties being separated, Donkin went away, and Pooley followed. An altercation ensued, which was followed up by another assault. Evidence was contradictory as to who was the aggressor in the second assault but the R.M. considered it proved that Pooley struck the first blow in both assaults. He imposed a fine of £5. Edward Pooley and Albert Bramhall (the latter a money-taker for the English cricketers) were then charged with wilfully and maliciously destroying clothes and plans, the property of Ralph Donkin. At 10.30 on the night of the assault, Donkin's bedroom at Warner's Hotel was seen to be in the usual order. Shortly after, Pooley was seen to come out of Donkin's bedroom and Bramhall was standing close to the door. At 11 o'clock, the waiter, whose suspicions were aroused, went into the bedroom and found Donkin's clothes and a lot of plans torn up. The damage to the clothes was valued at £35; the damage to the plans at £60. The bench committed both men for trial. Bail was accepted - each man in his personal surety of £200, and two sureties of £100 each.

Six weeks later, they were acquitted by the Supreme Court at Christchurch. Local generosity overflowed. A whip-round produced £50 and a gold watch.[233]

Meanwhile, a Pooley-less England continued their tour of Australia. There were not many rest days between the two Test Matches, as they took themselves off to play at the Back Creek at Bendigo against Twenty-two of that gold-mining town, then at Ballarat and Ararat. Haygarth notes blandly that "E Pooley did not play for England"[234].

In mid-April, they played against Twenty-two of South Australia, their twenty third and last match in Australia, to say nothing of the the eight they had played in New Zealand. Of cricket's reference books, only *Lillywhite's Cricketers' Companion* has any reference to the cause of Pooley's detachment from his colleagues.

---

[233] Ross *The Surrey Story* pp 28-9
[234] *S & B* Vol XIV pp 23 & 26

On April 19 they left Glenelg, homeward bound and on June 2 arrived in London safe and sound, without Pooley who reached home at a later date....
Pooley was absent owing to a charge of wilful damage from which he was subsequently honourably acquitted.[235]

It was July 9 1877 before Pooley arrived back in England. His second child and eldest daughter by Minnie Sabine, Alice Minnie, had been born in Battersea on 10 April. He had missed the birth and most of the pregnancy.

---

[235] 1878 edition p 23

WBCZ 003622

Registration Number KC006955

REGISTRATION DISTRICT COSBARTH COFRESTRU	Chepstow

1842. BIRTH in the Sub-district of GENEDIGAETH yn Is-ddosbarth Chepstow in the County of Monmouth & Gloucester

Columns: Colofau:	1	2	3	4	5	6	7	8	9	10
No Rhif	When and where born Pryd a lle'r ganwyd	Name if any Enw os oes un	Sex Rhyw	Name and surname of father Enw a chyfenw'r tad	Name, surname and maiden surname of mother Enw, cyfenw a chyfenw morwynol y fam	Occupation of father Gwaith y tad	Signature, description and residence of informant Llofnod, disgrifiad a chyfeiriad yr hysbysydd	When registered Pryd y cofrestrwyd	Signature of registrar Llofnod y cofrestrydd	Name entered after registration Enw a roddwyd ar ôl cofrestru
446	Fourteenth of February 1842 Chepstow	Edward William	Boy	William Pooly	Harriet Pooly formerly farmer	School Master	Wm Pooly Fabr Chepstow	Third of Harch 1842	B.M.Dakal Registrar	

1   Copy of Edward William Pooley's Birth Certificate explodes the Myths of a hundred years

Lower Church st., Chepstow   K.Waters

2   Pooley's birthplace, Lower Church Street, Chepstow [Courtesy of
the artist, Mrs Mercedes Waters]

3   The site of Myrtle Cottage, where William Pooley, Edward's father,
was a schoolmaster.

Chepstow Cricket Club.

1838.

President,—COL. LEWIS.

LIST OF MEMBERS.

1.	Baker, John	Chepstow	21.	M'Carthy, Felix	Chepstow
2.	Baldwyn, J. Lewis	ditto	22.	Morris, John	ditto
3.	Birt, John	Mounton	23.	Morris, Trevor, M.D.	ditto
4.	Bradford, B. M.	Chepstow	24.	Matthews, Rev. T. A.	ditto
5.	Cheese, James	ditto	25.	Peele, Wm. Henry	Aylesmore
6.	Carruthers, David	The Grondra	26.	Purchas, R. N.	Chepstow
7.	Curre, Edward M.	Itton Court	27.	Richman, Richard	St. Briavels
8.	Carter, Edwin	Chepstow	28.	Rosser, 'John	Chepstow
9.	Evans, James	ditto	29.	Sayce, Rev. Henry	Crick
10.	Evans, Thomas	ditto	30.	Sayce, George	ditto
11.	Fenton, Charles	Stroat	31.	Snead, John Best	Chepstow
12.	Gilbert, James	St. Arvans	32.	Sandford, Stephen	ditto
13.	Memfray, Rev. R.	Chepstow	33.	Toye, William E.	ditto
14.	Jenkins, Thomas B.	ditto	34.	Williams, Sir Edm. K.C.B.	Portskewett
15.	Jeukins, R. C.	Beachley	35.	Wise, Henry	Caldicot
16.	Jones, John	Chepstow	36.	Woodroffe, Samuel, jun.	Chepstow
17.	Kirby, Edwin D.	ditto	37.	Wall, Edward R.	ditto
18.	Lewis, Col. Thomas	St. Pierre	38.	Wetherhead, Thos.	ditto
19.	Lewis, Charles J.	ditto	39.	Westley, E. P.	ditto
20.	Lewis, George	Chepstow			

COMMITTEE MEMBERS.

1. Mr. E. Curre		4. Mr. Matthews	
2. Mr. T. Jenkins		5. Mr. James Evans	
3. Mr. J. Morris			

J. B. SNEAD, Treasurer.

J. L. BALDWYN, Sec.

1 - List of members for 1838 (Additions represent 1839's new members).

4   Chepstow Cricket Club - 1838 membership list with 1839's new members added in manuscript. They include William Pooley (between 26 and 27) [Chepstow Cricket Club]

5   4 Shepperton Cottages, Islington where the Pooley family lived in the 1840s

6   22 The Green Richmond: the Schoolhouse, now occupied by management consultants, SDG

7   Richmond Green where Pooley learned his cricket and his gambling

8   'The Cricketers', Richmond Green, where he learned his drinking

For 1861, the annual meeting of the Club, was held on 18 April, at which the office-bearers for the previous season were all re-elected. Fourteen gentlemen at this meeting and fifteen, at two subsequently held, were received into the membership; & the committee were instructed to look out for a professional, provided a sufficient sum was received for that purpose. At another meeting a letter was read from Chas Lawrence, Dublin, who had been written to in regard to a prof—, stating that he could recommend one at 35/ per week, & travelling expences." It was decided to accept the services of this person; but —as previously noticed —he was engaged for Col. Buchanan, Drumpellier before the Perth Club could secure him. Mr. Jno. Lillywhite, however, who had been written to, was on the outlook for a bowler, and had his eye on one Chatterton; but he was also placed elsewhere. In writing, Lillywhite says: — "I have therefore engaged Pooley, a Surrey man, who played in the Surrey Colts match. He was bowling to me the other day at Harrow School & gave satisfaction. He will leave here on Tuesday." Pooley's term with the Perth Club extended over seven weeks, at £2 per week, costing the club —with travelling expences —fully £20, which was raised by special subscriptions. For this season there were 45 ordinary subscribers, £25 who subscribed specially for a bowler, the money for the year; amounting to nearly £46. The principal subscribers to the special fund of which we speak, were Messrs. A.F. Moultrie, Geo Condie, R. Walker, W. McLeish, J.F. Halket, H. Hooke, Jno. Thomas, Jas Imrie, J.A. Imrie, R.C.L. Blair, W. Ross, Joseph Smith &c. Pooley's services to the Club in 1861, were entirely satisfactory. It need hardly be mentioned, that since then, he has figured very prominently in the cricket world; especially as cricket-keeper to the U.S. of England Eleven.

9   Pooleys first professional appointment - Perth 1861.
From *History of Perth Cricket Club* by William Sievwright.
[Courtesy of Perth Museum & Art Gallery (Archive 479),
Perth and Kinross Council, Scotland]

CERTIFIED COPY OF AN ENTRY OF MARRIAGE

GIVEN AT THE GENERAL REGISTER OFFICE

Application Number W 010 212 .

1862. Marriage solemnized at *[Parish Church]* .... in the County of ....

No.	When Married	Name and Surname	Age	Condition	Rank or Profession	Residence at the time of Marriage	Father's Name and Surname	Rank or Profession of Father
404	29th August 1862	Edward William Pooley	22	Bachelor	Servant	Burslem	Barton Bird William Pooley	Shoemaker
		Ellen Hunt	20	Spinster	—	Hanley	Edmund Hunt (Servant)	Hunt

Married in the *Parish Church* according to the Rites and Ceremonies of the Established Church by ....

Edward William Pooley   William Pooley
Ellen Hunt   Emily Edmund Hunt, Registrar

CERTIFIED to be a true copy of an entry in the certified copy of a register of Marriages in the Registration District of Newington ...
Given at the GENERAL REGISTER OFFICE, under the Seal of the said Office, the 9th day of November 1999

MXA 539181

This certificate is issued in pursuance of section 65 of the Marriage Act 1949. Sub-section 3 of that section provides that any certified copy of an entry purporting to be sealed or stamped with the seal of the General Register Office shall be received as evidence of the marriage to which it relates without any further or other proof of the entry, and no certified copy purporting to have been given in the said Office shall be of any force or effect unless it is sealed or stamped as aforesaid.

CAUTION: THERE ARE OFFENCES RELATING TO FALSIFYING OR ALTERING A CERTIFICATE AND USING OR POSSESSING A FALSE CERTIFICATE © CROWN COPYRIGHT

WARNING: A CERTIFICATE IS NOT EVIDENCE OF IDENTITY.

10 Copy of Certificate of Pooley's marriage to Ellen Hunt, 25 March 1863

11   Amelia Street, Newington, where he began his brief married life

12   2 Barford Terrace, Islington, where in 1864, Pooley had a "cricket and cigar store" and where his first child, Ellen, was born. The premises are now 72 Liverpool Road and a Tandoori Restaurant

13   5ft 6in of aggression

Cricket Match played at _Bruman_ between _The North of Ireland C.C._

First Innings

No.	Name of the Batsman	Figures as Scored	How Out	Bowler's Name	Runs
1	Hampton	1141	c L.S.P.Trifali	Henderson	7
2	Capt. Jones	11,1412,11,2113	b	H. Hunter	19
3	Capt. Brown	11131	b	Hunter	9
4	Pooley	011121143,2111121	b	Hunter	14
5	Capt. Bland	1111	c & b	Cordum	4
6	W.F. Ashton	3	b	Stilgoe	3
7	a. B. Bright..ll		b	Cordum	0
8	Major Lettsom	2431	b	Cordum	10
9	H. Houghton	11	b	Hunter	7
10	J.R. McCullogh		run out		0
11	J.C. Clarke		not out		0
	Byes	12,12,2,11,1,1,1,2,1			22
	Leg Byes	12			1
	Wide Balls	1111			1
	No Balls	111		Total of First Innings	121

Runs at the fall of each wicket: 1 for 21 · 2 for 44 · 3 for 55 · 4 for 75 · 5 for 81 · 6 for 94 · 7 for 105 · 8 for 118 · 9 for 120 · 10 for 121

Second Innings

No.	Name of the Batsman	Figures as Scored	How Out	Bowler's Name	Runs
1	Capt. Jones	1	b	Hunter	1
2	Pooley	42,4,2,1,11,2,2,2,1,21,1,4,1	c Cordum	Henderson	39
3	Lieut. Saville		b	Cordum	0
4	Hampton	112,113,11,1,1	b	Cordum	21
5	Capt. Brown	1,3,1,1	b	Henderson	11
6	W.F. Ashton	11	b	Henderson	3
7	Capt. Bland	112	b	Henderson	4
8	H. Houghton	1	c Cordum	Henderson	1
9	a. B. Brighdull	31	b	Cordum	4
10	Capt. Clarke		b	Cordum	0
11	J. Mc Cullogh		not out		0
	Byes	1111			4
	Leg Byes	122			1
	Wide Balls				
	No Balls			Total Second Innings	93

Total of the two Innings

Runs at the fall of each wicket: 1 for 18 · 2 for 19 · 3 for 47 · 4 for 74 · 5 for 79 · 6 for 84 · 7 for 87 · 8 for 93 · 9 for 93 · 10 for 93

PUBLISHED BY FREDERICK LILLYWHITE, AT No 16, KENNINGTON OVAL.   LILLYWHITE'S GUIDE TO C

14   Pooley dominates club cricket in Belfast

v. The Garrison (with Heighn & Pooley) on May 20th 18/1865

	Name of the Batsman	Figures as Scored	How Out	Bowler's Name	Run
1	J. M. Sinclair		c. Bland	Heighn	16
2	W. Ewing	4111	L. B. W.	Pooley	6
3	L. S. P. Filgate	1	b	Pooley	1
4	J. Hunter	2311	b	Pooley	8
5	C. Stilson	41121	b	Heighn	10
6	C. K. Cordesan	1133	L. B. W.	Heighn	2
7	R. H. Barr		b	Pooley	32
8	Lord Massereene	2111	ct. Bland	Pooley	7
9	Ed. Henderson	131211	ct. Jones	Pooley	9
10	J. Connor b	1	b	Heighn	1
11	J. Filgate	1	not out		1
	Byes	11			2
	Leg Byes	1311			4
	Wide Balls				
	No Balls				
				Total of First Innings	113

Runs at the fall of each Wicket	1 for 4	2 for 13	3 for 31	4 for 31	5 for 50	6 for 69	7 for 99	8 for 111	9 for 111	10 for 113

Order of going in .... Second Innings

	Name	Figures	How Out	Bowler	Run
1	J. M. Sinclair		ct. & b.	Heighn	0
2	W. Ewing	1	ct. McCullough	Heighn	1
3	Ed. Henderson	11	b	Heighn	4
4	R. H. Barr	3	ct. Osmer	Pooley	3
5	Lord Massereene	212113	ct. Bland	Pooley	13
6	C. K. Cordesan	331	L. B. W	Heighn	7
7	L. S. P. Filgate	1131	b	Pooley	7
8	J. Filgate	311	b	Heighn	5
9	J. Hunter	1131	not out		6
10	J. Connor b	23	b	Pooley	5
11	C. Stilson		absent		0
	Byes	2			2
	Leg Byes	3			3
	Wide Balls				
	No Balls				
	Total of the Two Innings			Total Second Innings	56

Runs at the fall of each Wicket	1 for 1	2 for 2	3 for 7	4 for 26	5 for 32	6 for 33	7 for 45	8 for 47	9 for 56	10 for 56

PUBLISHED BY FREDERICK LILLYWHITE, AT N° 18, KENNINGTON OVAL.   LILLYWHITE'S GUIDE TO

[North of Ireland Cricket and Football Club]

15   Lambeth Police Court, now the Jamyang Buddhist Temple

16   With the United South of England XI c1870. Pooley is on the extreme left

17   Wick Road, Teddington, where Pooley lived in 1884 with his common law wife, Minnie Sabine, and growing illegitimate family

18   Fulwell Road, Teddington, where he lived in 1888, the birth place of his eighth child, Alfred

19   Rowton House, Bond Street (now the Centrepoint Vauxhall Hostel and Job Centre, Bondway), Vauxhall: Pooley's last home, apart from the Workhouse

20   Renfrew Road Workhouse, Lambeth

21   The Workhouse Infirmary and neglected grounds

REGISTRATION DISTRICT _Kensington_

1907. DEATH in the Sub-district of _Kensington_ .... in the _County of London_

Columns:-	1	2	3	4	5	6	7	8	9
No.	When and where died	Name and surname	Sex	Age	Occupation	Cause of death	Signature, description and residence of informant	When registered	Signature of registrar
134	Eighteenth July 1907 Workhouse Infirmary Marloes Street	Edward Pooley	Male	4 years	Orphaned inmate of workhouse Gore Street Kensington	Acute illness Gastro-enteritis Asthenia Pleur Certified by J.A.R.... MD	E. Davis Steward Workhouse Infirmary Gore Street	Twenty sixth July 1907	Whitworth Registrar

CERTIFIED to be a true copy of an entry in the certified copy of a Register of Deaths in the District above mentioned.
Given at the GENERAL REGISTER OFFICE, under the Seal of the said Office, the ....12th............day of.....February.....19 08.

DXZ 450318

See note overleaf

22   The end of it all.....copy of Pooley's death certificate

23   The new generation......Michael (great grandson), Ronald (grandson)
and Natalie (great granddaughter)

CHAPTER 9

THE TWILIGHT YEARS
(1877/83)

By the time Pooley arrived back in England after the 1876/77 tour of the Antipodes, there was not a great deal of the 1877 season left. He was now aged 35 and the best of his playing career was already behind him. The face of cricket was changing: the days of Single Wicket and Given Men were almost over, the professional United South of England XI had fewer fixtures and would cease to exist after 1882. For a fixture against Eighteen of Keighley they were billed in the *Keighley Herald* as Surrey and Sussex as it was thought this would be a greater attraction. The match was not covered in detail by any newspaper other than the local one.

County cricket was in its ascendancy; serious international cricket had begun in Australia the previous winter and the Australians were to tour England in 1878, but Edward Pooley, though still producing competent performances, was never again to reach the heights of performance of the late sixties and early seventies. Now batting in the lower order, he only just managed a double figure first-class batting average. The decline had begun; in his first innings on his return from New Zealand, he made a duck at Trent Bridge. He appeared for England against Gloucestershire, the first time England had played a county for eleven years. Gloucestershire were clearly up to it as they won by five wickets. Pooley had 1 and 17, two catches and three stumpings, but his season is perhaps epitomised by one comment in *Wisden* on the match against Middlesex at The Oval, "Pooley was out for 16, a little innings that included a big hit for 5."[236] There were one or two highlights and notable feats, but these were now more scattered. He did not play in the Gentlemen v Players fixture or feature at the Canterbury Festival. For both Pooley and Surrey, the season was, to borrow a phrase he might at another time have brought with him from Australia, "pretty ordinary". *Wisden's* report on Surrey wicket-keeping during 1877 is leaden and factual:

---

[236] *Wisden* 1878 p 146

E Pooley kept wicket in 9 matches; he stumped 13 and caught out 16; Mr W Abbott kept in 3 matches; he stumped 2 and caught out 7: F Pooley kept in one match; he caught out one; and Jupp kept in one match.[237]

The Pooley decline was, of course relative; his batting was certainly less effective, but there was never any doubt about his ability to hold his place in the Surrey Eleven and in a season free of injuries, suspensions and criminal proceedings, he and Barratt were the only two players to appear in all fourteen Surrey matches in 1878

With The Oval crowds he remained as popular as ever and retained his ability to rise to an occasion. When Surrey entertained the Australian tourists in June, the huge attendance put some pressure - literally and metaphorically - on the ground facilities. Even allowing for the hyperbole of *Wisden*'s Victorian prose, it was clearly an appropriate occasion to which to rise.

NEVER BEFORE OR SINCE HAS THERE BEEN SO MANY PEOPLE ON THE OVAL at a cricket match as were gathered, crowded and crushed together on that now memorable Monday, the third of June 1878 to witness the Australians commence their match against the Surrey Eleven. Fortunately the weather was gloriously fine, and the sight that afternoon on the Oval was truly "wonderful". Before the time arrived for the commencement of play over 2000 had paid their 1s for admission; from then the people streamed on to the ground so continuously that by luncheon time it was calculated there were 10,000 present; still the cry was "they come" and in such thoroughly unmanageable crowds did they "come" that a semi-official notice on the following day stated "A little later the resources of the Club were sorely taxed by hundreds still waiting for admission, and as the carriage gates had been once broken down by the expectant mass outside, several new entrances were made for the purposes of relieving the pressure." Such was the exciting state of affairs outside the ground; inside the throng was simply marvellous in the numbers, the pavilion seats and steps were chock full; the spacious rows of seats, dignified by the title of "Grand Stand", were literally packed with people, who willingly parted with extra coin to obtain the "coign of advantage" that those seats certainly gave; the little terraced embankment, that so happily hides the hideously ugly "Skating Rink", was crowded to inconvenience, and all around the cricketers, sat and stood a ring of people so dense that in more than one part it was computed that they were crowded together 20 deep, and the whole numbers present at 6 o'clock that day were supposed by Bell's Life to have been close on 20,000.

---

[237] Ib   p 151

Spofforth, who finished the first innings with 27-10-52-8 was clearly an attraction, but so, batting at 7, was local hero Ted Pooley.

Pooley was next man in, and to the evident delight of the thousands present Pooley was "in form"....Pooley then saw three Surrey men come and go, as at 81 both Strachan and Barratt left, and at 83, Jones was bowled. Southerton was next man in, and as he and Pooley increased the Surrey score from 83 to three figures, so increased the cheering for Surrey, until at a quarter to 2, Boyle bowled Pooley for 29; then the innings ended for 107 runs, Southerton, not out, 13.....
Spofforth having taken 8 of the wickets - 5 bowled, and Gregory having caught 3 at slip
Pooley stumped Horan for 16, at 38 Pooley caught out A Bannerman, at 58 Pooley stumped Spofforth. [238]

Statistically, Pooley's best wicket-keeping performance of 1878 was against Kent at The Oval when he caught two and stumped eight. Statistics can, however, be misleading. In a way, what happened was a mirror image of declaration bowling, which can also distort statistics. At the time declarations were not permitted and to give themselves time to bowl Surrey out, Kent deliberately threw their wickets away in the second innings. Pooley went along with it for a while, then declined to put the wicket down when Harris deliberately attempted to throw his wicket away.[239] Professionalism played professionalism. Not for another decade was provision for declaring an innings closed introduced into the Laws - and then only on the third day.

Meanwhile, Pooley played once again for England against Gloucestershire, but without distinction [240] (seven runs and two stumpings) as well as a handful of matches for the USEE. He also umpired the Surrey Club v Surrey Colts match[241], a sure sign that the end was in sight.

1879 was one of the wettest summers on record [242], Pooley recorded the lowest batting average of his career (7.35 - 125 in 17 completed innings), notwithstanding 37 not out against Kent. It was the last year of the Southerton-Pooley combination. Southerton was now aged 51 and in his

---

[238]   Ib   1879 p 123
[239]   Lord Harris *History of Kent County Cricket* pp 73 & 446
        S & B Vol XIV p 840
[240]   *Wisden* 1879 p 135
[241]   *S & B* Vol XIV p
[242]   *Wisden* 1880 p 47

twenty-sixth season. Against Somersetshire (so-called at the time), the roundarm off-spinner bowled through the innings for 46.3-17-60-7, Pooley catching three and stumping one. Ten days earlier a benefit match had been played for him at The Oval - North v South, the usual benefit fixture in those days, drawing from *Wisden* the two-edged comment, undoubtedly intended as a compliment, but exposing the divisions of cricket and society at the time, that he was "always civil to those who occupy a superior social position to himself"[243]. He died the following summer.

1880 was a significant year for English cricket. The first Test Match on English soil was played at The Oval, but the club whose home ground that was had another poor season, winning only two matches. They contrived to be all out for 16 against Notts at The Oval (Their lowest on the ground and their lowest anywhere until 1993 when Essex bowled them out for 14 at Chelmsford) and Yorkshire beat them by an innings and 123 runs, having recorded the highest total of the season by a county - 398.

The Yorkshire match was one in which Pooley put on a brave, single-handed batting performance, not out 15 batting at 9 in the first innings and, opening in the follow on, his first half-century for four years. No one else scored above 15.

Little need be said of Surrey's first innings. No stand was made until Read joined Humphrey when the score which then stood at 43 was raised to 125 before a separation was effected. Pooley hit hard but neither Potter nor Blamires could assist him...With 222 to score to save a single innings defeat, Surrey followed on at 6.20 and by 7 o'clock had made 7 for the loss of one wicket (Mr Wyld's), Pooley being not out 0. On Saturday Surrey suffered a most crushing defeat, being beaten by an innings and 123 runs. Pooley played with the utmost pluck and dash, more than half his runs being made by 4's, but Hill's bowling played such havoc with the other Surrey wickets that no one could render him material help. Hill accomplished the "hat-trick", taking the last three wickets with successive balls.[244]

Seven years later, Surrey would for the first of two occasions in their history dominate the county scene. But that was for the future. In those early eighties, the wilderness years continued.

---

[243] Ib   p 157
[244] Ib   p 139

In one respect there was some ground for hope, in that the committee showed a determination to give young players the preference over those who have seen their best day, and in some case the County team, owing to the infusion of youth and activity, showed a smartness in the field which certainly had been wanting for some years past[245]

As Pooley ended his second decade with Surrey, he would have to be counted among those who had seen their best day. W W Read, one of the most prolific batsmen of the era had arrived on the scene and the previous season had scored 338 against Oxford University. The writing was on the wall. The frisky colt of the sixties had become the old war-horse of the eighties. The next generation was knocking at the door and *Wisden* was able to refer to "the good form shown by the Colt Abel.[246]

Mr W W Read was able to play in every match, and proved the mainstay of the Surrey batting, beside showing exceptional form as a wicket-keeper[247]

But if Pooley's life as a cricketer was over, it was two years before he would lie down - and his spectre would haunt the committee for as many years as he had been associated with the club as a player.

1880 was an important year for English cricket, but it also represented something of a watershed in Pooley's own life. On 2 June, his father died suddenly of a heart attack[248]. Edward missed the next two matches at Trent Bridge and Old Trafford. It is likely that his association with Minnie Sabine, to whom a third child by Edward, John Harold, had been born in February, as well as his alleged misdemeanours in The Oval refreshment bar, at Sheffield and at Christchurch, had caused something of a strain in the internal relations of a respectable Victorian professional family, but there is no evidence yet of the complete schism that was to occur before the end of the century. The inquest on his father's death was held on 5 June and as the eldest surviving son, Edward, in all probability, was in attendance.

Two weeks later on 16 June, James Southerton, his accomplice in almost half his dismissals, also departed this life.

[245] Lillywhite's *Cricketers' Annual* 1882 p 90
[246] *Wisden* 1883 p 150
[247] Ib 1882 p 165
[248] William Pooley's death certificate

...the greatest misfortune was that when death claimed James Southerton on the 16th of June, and thereby deprived Surrey of the services of one of the most successful bowlers that ever appeared in the ranks of the County Eleven, and one of the most straightforward, popular, intelligent, respectful and deserving cricketers that ever put on flannels. [249]

He was in his fifty-third year. At 49 years 119 days on the Ides of March 1877, he was and remains the oldest cricketer to make a Test début. He was also the first Test cricketer to die. His first record is unlikely to be beaten; his second never will be. So, within two weeks, Edward had lost two important influences on his cricketing career, if not necessarily on his lifestyle. His descent into solitude was not too far ahead.

His top score in seven matches in 1881 was "an exceedingly useful 36" against Middlesex[250], but he had only nine catches and three stumpings. Read had 4 and 6, Carmichael 2 and 3. No longer certain of his place in the side, he was appointed scorer for the matches at Maidstone, Brighton and Clifton at a sum of £3.[251]

But in 1882 he was back to play in 19 first-class matches. Now batting regularly in the lower order, he made a pair against the Australians at The Oval. The popularity of the game and of the Australians was demonstrated by the fact that several hundred turned up for the third day, despite the visitors requiring only 21 to win with eight wickets standing.

Pooley improved only slightly on his batting performance when he appeared against the Australians again for a United Eleven at Chichester in June, being not out 1 and stumped for 0. The Australians made 501 and the United Eleven pusillanimously replied with 166 and 72. With a stumping and two catches Pooley helped W G Grace and Gilbert dispose of Bannerman, Horan and Blackham. When the two sides met again at Tunbridge Wells, immediately after The Oval Test Match which gave birth to The Ashes, Pooley made 2, but still continued to make an impression behind the wicket.

---

[249]   Ib   1881 p 127
[250]   Ib   p 180
[251]   SCCC mins 21 July 1881 SCRO 2042/1/4

A smart catch at the wicket sent back Horan at 38 and in the following over Murdoch ran out to drive Parnham, missed the ball and was easily stumped....Blackham was taken at the wicket.[252]

The match ended in a rain-affected draw.

In between, Pooley had made his thirty-second and final first-class fifty, exactly 50 not out against Kent at The Oval.

Pooley, when the Kentish bowling was fairly collared, let out in quite his old style. [253]

Pooley carried out his bat for a plucky and capital 50. [254]

and his wicket-keeping was contributing to the occasional win. Against Middlesex at The Oval, "Until Mr Scott's dismissal a win for Middlesex seemed certain".[255] Surrey won by 25 runs, Scott being st Pooley b Barratt 126.

Against Sussex at Brighton

Pooley's wicket-keeping too deserves special praise. In the second innings of Sussex he had a hand in the downfall of five batsmen, three caught and two stumped[256]

In his last full season, Pooley took 22 catches and had the same number of stumpings, including 17 of each for Surrey for whom he had played in all fourteen county matches, plus the two University matches.

Pooley kept wicket in excellent form in all the matches [257], although in the Lancashire match at The Oval, Pooley who was very lame, was not at his best at the wicket. [258]

Crown Prince Walter William would have to wait another half season before he could inherit King Edward William's place behind the stumps. The Club

[252] *Wisden* 1883 p 274
[253] *Cricket* 1882 p 201
[254] *Wisden* 1883 pp127-8
[255] *Cricket* 1882 p 63
[256] Ib p138
[257] *Wisden* 1883 p 115
[258] *Cricket* 1882 p 249

agreed to award him a benefit in 1883. *Wisden*'s observations were suitably laudatory, if not entirely accurate.

POOLEY'S LONG AND INVALUABLE SERVICES FOR SURREY are to be recognised in the coming season. At the time of printing this part of "Wisden's" the match and the days on which it would be played are not fixed, but the most attractive contest of the season at the Oval would certainly be the fittest to select for "Teddy's" benefit, and in the present flourishing state of the Surrey exchequer there is no doubt that the right match will be chosen. No professional is more popular, and if length of service and brilliant doings are to count, no man better deserves three days of splendid weather, three full days of first-class cricket, a crowded ground and a well-filled subscription list.
Pooley's introduction into the Surrey XI dates from 1865 and anything less than an exceedingly brief list of his best performances at the wicket would fill far more space than can be allocated in this book. His most successful season behind the sticks was probably that of 1868 when *he captured no fewer than 63 wickets,* stumping 33 and catching out 30. About his best season's batting there can be no doubt as in 1870, *he headed the batting list* with an aggregate of 771 runs, and an average of 24.27 for 34 innings in three of which he was not out, his highest score that year being 94. In that year too he accomplished the great wicket-keeping feat of *taking 6 wickets in one innings.* [259]

Calculated now, that batting average would read 24.87: *Wisden* at the time was still giving both batting and bowling averages as an integer and "number over". Pooley's début was, of course, in 1861, not 1865 and there is no mention of his world record of 12 victims in a match, nor of his only first-class century in 1871, indicative of the fact that statistical accuracy and consciousness of records were to belong to a future era. 1871, 1873, 1874 and 1881 are mentioned as years when, owing to damaged hands, he kept in few matches. The writer appears to have conveniently forgotten that his few appearances in 1873 were attributable to totally different reasons.

Away from the first-class scene it was in May 1882 that Pooley had returned to his birth-place, Chepstow, to appear against Twenty-Two of Chepstow and District for a "United XI of All England" - effectively the USEE, as none of the other professional touring sides were any longer in existence. [260] On this occasion with W G Grace absent, the team was captained by his elder brother, E M and supplemented by non-southerner and Derbyshire professional, Jack Platts, who contributed a useful 143, followed by 10 for 63 in the second innings, but still found himself on the losing side.

---

[259] *Wisden* 1883 p 216
[260] Sissons *The Players* p 62

It seems barely credible that Pooley was unaware that he was returning to his birthplace. His father had been there for something like nine years and though Edward had been an infant when the family left, his eldest sister, Maria had been perhaps six years of age and must have had memories of it. There would surely, at some time, have been family talk about their time in Chepstow, unless, as I suggested in the opening chapter, Thomas's death had caused them deliberately and consciously to exclude it from all conversations.

The local press, which would in all likelihood have scented a "return of the native" story had it been aware of it, mentions simply that "the most noticeable feature in the play of the Eleven was that of the veteran player Pooley for 35".[261] It refers to the second innings, the scorecard of the match actually says 23 not out at no 9 (They were two players short!) from a total of 47 - part of a contribution which included 5 not out in the first innings, two catches and two stumpings. The match itself was an extraordinary one. England batted first and scored 268. Chepstow replied with 141 and 193 in the follow on. This left the Eleven 67 to win on the third day

which was considered a comparatively easy task, the prevailing opinion being that the match would terminate in an easy victory for the strangers, they appearing so confident that neither E M Grace nor W J Hughes put in an appearance leaving their colleagues to settle the matter, but the result proved to the contrary, for they succeeded in putting together 47 only, thus leaving the local team victors by 19 runs.[262]

It was the Eleven's only defeat in five matches that summer.

Back on the larger stage, the match chosen for Pooley's benefit in 1883 was the North v South fixture at The Oval on Thursday, Friday and Saturday, 21, 22 and 23 June. He himself did not play and the North won a close match by 22 runs - 130 and 215 against 181 and 142.

The weather was not of a desirable kind on the opening day, but, nevertheless, Pooley had no reason to be dissatisfied with the result as, in addition to the sum of £400 18s taken at the gates during the three days the match occupied, he had a very fair subscription list to which the Surrey Club contributed £25, and the

---

[261] *Chepstow Cricket Club* p 11quoting *Chepstow Weekly Advertiser*
[262]   Ib   p 12

MCC £15. A pleasant incident in connection with the match was the presentation, during the interval on the second day of a cheque for £250 and an artistically illuminated inscription of vellum to Mr W W Read in recognition of his brilliant batting in Australia as a member of the Hon Ivo Bligh's team.

£250 and a piece of vellum for an average of 32.57 over a four Test series, against £400 and a subscription list for 23 years cricket. Such was the distinction between amateur and professional in Victorian England.

None the less, £400 at a time when the income of almost 90% of the population was below £100 per annum[263] was not to be sneezed at and was perhaps worth something approaching a six-figure sum in late twentieth century equivalent terms.

In 1884, Pooley is recorded in Lillywhite's *Cricketers' Companion* as living at Fairfield Cottage, Hampton Wick, a property possibly acquired with his benefit fund. So Edward Pooley, his cricket career over, settled down to a comfortable, roses-round-the-door retirement in his country cottage. But those "faults of a private character" were not long dormant and after what seems to have been a period of relative affluence in the Teddington and Twickenham area, ten years later, his life had become merely existence, purposeless and aimless.

His immediate family had left Richmond by 1861. In 1866, 22 The Green was occupied by a Mr Frederick Pigott, the neighbouring properties, 19-21 and 23-25 all lodging houses. John Faithfull was landlord of *The Cricketers* at no 24.[264] By 1871, no 22 stood unoccupied.[265] After William's death, some of the family moved to Battersea: Harriet is recorded in the 1881 Census of Population as residing at 363 Battersea Park Road where, along with her younger son, Frederick, she is described as a tobacconist. Living with them are Annie, Harriet's elder sister, now aged 70 and according to the 'Occupation' column, formerly a dressmaker. She had been living with the family forty years earlier in Chepstow, but not thirty years earlier in Richmond. So one can only surmise that during the Richmond period, she stayed on in Chepstow or elsewhere with her mother, Elizabeth, then after the latter's death, followed her sister to London and again lived with her sister and other members of the family. Also resident at 363 Battersea Park

[263] Sir Derek Birley *A Social History of English Cricket* p 106
[264] *Post Office Directory of the Home Counties Vol II Kent, Surrey, Sussex 1866*
[265] 1861 and 1871 Census of Population

Road is Ellen Pooley, aged 17, described as a niece of Harriet[266], though in fact a niece of Frederick and Edward's elder daughter by his now defunct marriage. Edward's married sister, Maria, was living just down the road at 8 Bullen Street where Harriet died in 1884, the year after Edward retired from professional cricket with a substantial benefit.

The houses in which they lived are no longer there, that part of Battersea Park Road now being occupied by Battersea Technology College and the high rise flats of the St James Grove Estate and although the odd-numbered houses remain in Bullen Street, the even numbered ones have been replaced by a car park and children's playground. Edward also was living in Battersea at 14 Beaufield Street, so we have a large, extended, but seemingly close-knit family which makes Edward's isolation from them a decade later all the more poignant.

There are, however, strong clues as to the reason for the schism in that 14 Beaufield Street entry, where Edward, now 39, has a "wife", Minnie aged 27, two sons and a daughter, Edward, John and Minnie, aged seven, one and four respectively. Additionally, there is Fanny, younger daughter of his marriage to Ellen, now aged 15 and a metal maker in a bell factory[267]. In an era where the behaviour of the Prince of Wales was the subject of scandal and caused Queen Victoria to exclude him from state functions, such an irregular family relationship was not consonant with the ideals of respectable Victorian middle-class society.

The relationship with Minnie Sabine, however, does seem to have been pretty stable: she and Edward remained together for at least twenty years and on both the 1881 and 1891 censuses, she describes herself as Minnie Pooley. The first four children of the union are registered as Sabine (Walter Henry, the fourth, was born in 1882), the last four as Pooley.

The Richmond link seems to have been severed on his return from the 1876/77 tour. Earlier in the 1870s, he had run the Albany Beer House in Kew Foot Road[268] and continued to live in the town but, after the tour, lived first in Battersea and later in Teddington and Twickenham; his association with Minnie seems to have begun about 1873, the year of his

---

[266] 1881 Census of Population
[267] Ib
[268] *Licensing World* 27 July 1907

suspension from the Surrey side following the Sheffield incident, but throughout the 1880s, the family had a somewhat itinerant existence and after Battersea in 1881, 1884 saw them at Wick Road, South Teddington[269] almost certainly the Fairfield Cottage, Hampton Wick, of *Lillywhite's Cricketers Companion.* Edward and his family never settled down in one place: his ten children were born in ten different houses and the addresses in Census of Population entries are different again.

For the 1883 season, Surrey expanded their programme by including fixtures with Derbyshire, Hampshire, Somersetshire [sic] and Leicestershire. The programme of Pooley, now aged 41, was, however, curtailed by age and injury and he did not play for Surrey after July.

Surrey's first appearance against one of the minor counties did not prove successful.

It was Leicestershire at Aylestone Road where the visitors lost by seven runs.

The Surrey Eleven was by no means representative, and in addition, Pooley injured his thumb, so that he was practically unable to bat, and Mr Read had to take the wicket.[270]

His last contribution to a Surrey victory was against Sussex at Brighton when Surrey won by two wickets.

When play ceased on Tuesday night Surrey had made 73 out of 136 wanted to win, with five of their best wickets down. Mainly, however, through the good batting of Pooley and Mr Horner, the runs were got yesterday with two wickets to fall.[271]

Horner made 14 not out, Pooley 18 not out. They were his last runs for Surrey. His final match was against Lancashire at Old Trafford, which he graced with one catch, two stumpings and a 'pair', c Payne b Barlow 0 and b Barlow 0.

He did have one more match, for Eleven of the South, against Eleven of the North on the Common at Tunbridge Wells, the fifth and last time the match

---

[269] Birth certificate of Charles Victor, 5th child and 4th son by Minnie Sabine
[270] *Cricket* 1883 p 115
[271] Ib p 246

was played on the ground. It was the last time Pooley played on any ground. He made 8 not out and 1 and took one catch as the final curtain fell on his cricketing career.

CHAPTER 10

THE SOCIAL CONTEXT - GENTLEMEN AND PLAYERS - POOLEY AND W G GRACE

There emerged, almost in direct descent from the old-time noblemen with their cricketing bailiffs and stewards, the device of 'players' and 'gentlemen'. That is a useful analogy, for the respected senior cricket 'pro' came to parallel, in manner and influence, the butler in the monied household or the sergeant major *apropos* the colonel.

.....The 'professionals' were working class, and a minute number were to enjoy extremely good fortune money-wise, whereas the 'amateurs' were middle and upper class, and several, not least W G Grace had to resort to shamateurism to support themselves...

The attempt to sustain a compromise 'share but not alike' policy was evident, so that, just as there were stalls for the toffs and the gallery for the plebs in the same theatre, or the paid and free pews in the same church and the public and saloon bars in the same pubs, there was the pavilion for gentlemen members and the terraces for working and lower middle class spectators and also the separate dressing rooms and pavilion gates for 'players' and 'gentlemen'.

This is how Eric Midwinter, cricket and social historian, colourfully describes the social background against which Edward Pooley played his cricket. [272] It was a time of above and below stairs, of the rich man in his castle and the poor man at his gate, a time when hierarchy, breeding, status and classification mattered, when class-distinctions were accepted almost without question. Sir Derek Birley sees both the cricketing and social scenes as zones of conflict rather than comfort.

The conflict in cricket between the independent professionals of the lower classes and the latter-day representatives of the old feudal system was thus part of a wider struggle. Before long, MCC, easy victors in their own little battle, had become smug about the turmoil afflicting the newer sports, but they achieved this complacent superiority only by the accident of time and with the help of extra large doses of hypocrisy. The need for hypocrisy had a lot to do with the Graces, and W.G. in particular, for he became a synonym for cricket and Britishness and perhaps the most famous and most hero-worshipped man in the country, but he made a nonsense of most of the emerging canons of the game. [273]

---

[272] *From Meadowland to Multinational Cricket Lore* Vol III Issue 4 January 1998
[273] Birley *A Social History of English Cricket* p 107

The whole social ethos is perhaps epitomised in the Canterbury Festival where Pooley was always such a popular attraction. The Ball Committee of fourteen for 1877 comprised two Lords, one Sir, four Esquires (one with three initials and one de C), three captains, one colonel and three majors. The Accounts show a donation of £50 to the Grace testimonial fund and, the following year, the wage bill for the cricketers came to £79 - two amateurs (W G and G F Grace at £10 each) seven professionals at £7 each and a further two at £5 each.[274]

By this time Pooley had ceased to be part of the occasion, but the social scene remained constant. The cricket itself, however, changed considerably over his seasons as a professional; the scene he joined in 1861 had some county cricket, but it did not dominate; the major fixtures were Gentlemen v Players, North v South, Eton v Harrow and Oxford v Cambridge. The expansion of the railway network enabled the professional touring elevens to flourish; amateur Fifteens, Eighteens, Twenty-twos and sundry other numbers were supplemented by "given men", professional cricketers were itinerant, bowling was underarm or roundarm and pitches rough and underprepared - if prepared at all. By the time he retired in 1883, the rudiments of a county championship were in place, international cricket was off the ground; the sun had set on the professional touring circuses, the rules on county qualification, by birth or residence were more tightly drawn, overarm bowling the norm and the heavy roller and pitch covering, if not yet general, had been implemented at Lord's in 1870 and 1872 respectively[275]. The social divisions were, however, as rigid as ever.

Certainly *The Times* in August 1857, exhibiting a chauvinism which would be frowned upon by advocates of political correctness today, had little doubt about the purpose of public schools cricket.

It is important to secure a race of young Englishmen who in days to come, shall retain the grasp of England on the world.

There were occasional exceptions to the two-tier class structure such as the Broughton Club in Manchester where there was minimal distinction between amateurs and professionals and members and the public[276], but the

274 Kent County Cricket Club minutes 20 July 1877   Centre for Kentish Studies
275 H S Altham *Dates in Cricket History* *Wisden* 1963 pp181-2
276 Rae *W G Grace; A Life* p 93

more typical model was neighbouring Old Trafford where until very recently traces of the old order still survived. The gentlemen-players distinction had formally disappeared, but there were other elements of divisiveness in separate dressing rooms for captain, capped players and uncapped players and restricted rights for lady members.

Major Philip Trevor in *The Problems of Cricket* in 1907, the year of Pooley's death, was advocating the abolition of the distinction between the professional and the amateur, but in general the social divisions were to remain virtually unchanged before the First World War, and it was not until 1963 that the Gentlemen-Players distinction was formally abolished and all became known as "cricketers". The attitude and approach to the game remained much the same.

Independently of greater freshness, there is another advantage that an Eleven of gentlemen have over an Eleven of players; the one side is playing freely and carelessly for its pleasure, the other is playing fearfully and nervously for a livelihood.
'Yes, it is very fair to laugh, gentlemen, among one another,' said a professional, 'when a player comes out without a run; but with us it is no laughing matter, for on a man's average depends his bread, and a few unlucky innings, especially before his name is well up, puts him out of the stream at once'. [277]

Pooley played with varying success in 25 Gentlemen v Players matches. There were generally three a year, at Lord's, The Oval and Brighton or Prince's in Chelsea, supplemented by Gentlemen of the South v Players of the South and an equivalent pairing in the north.

His first appearance was in 1866 when, in four innings, he failed to make double figures. He compensated the following season, however, with 85 at The Oval, his highest score of the season and his highest score in a Gentlemen v Players match.

The 1869 match at The Oval was the one on which E H Pickering's report ultimately landed Pooley in the Lambeth Police Court and was one of the closest, the Gentlemen ultimately winning by 17 runs. According to Old Ebor, there was something of a controversy when "just before the finish Willsher entered the field with a drink for Pooley, and it was then said that it was done for the purpose of wasting time." Pooley denied this, stating that

---

[277] Rev James Pycroft *Cricketana* p127

he and Wootton were going for the win anyway, even though they were 87 runs short when the ninth wicket fell. Actually it was 60. When Pooley was bowled by Absolom with minutes to spare, the Players were 17 short.[278]

It seems to have been an entertaining partnership. Using available contemporary sources, Joe Webber reports that, having driven W G for 5,

Pooley hit Buchanan for 3 in his next over, then he played one to the on side and ran. Maitland fielded the ball, threw at the wicket, missed, and an additional four were counted for the overthrow[279]

In every season but two, until 1879, Pooley was the regular wicket-keeper for the Players; the exceptions were 1877, which his adventures in New Zealand caused to be foreshortened, and 1873, the year of his suspension when it may be no more than coincidence that the Gentlemen won all three matches by an innings.

However 1874 saw the Players first win since 1866, Pooley's 39 not out contributing to a two wicket victory at Lord's. In all probability, he was among the most vociferous appealers involved in the "incident" in the third match of that season when G F Grace hit the ball back to Lillywhite for an easy chance but elder brother W G *palpably baulked the bowler*. The rejection of the appeal for obstruction was "not received with equanimity by the Players".[280]

whose misfortune in this match was that nearly every appeal by a Gentleman was decided affirmatively, and the Players' appeals were mainly met with NOT OUT. [281]

On 123 occasions, Pooley played with or against W G Grace - who "found cricket a country pastime and left it a national institution"[282] - 45 with and 88 against; 'with' for the USEE, the South, etc and against in Gentlemen v Players and their regional equivalent and Surrey v Gloucestershire[283] and perhaps nothing epitomised better the 'share but not alike' ethos to which

---

[278] Pullin *Talks with Old English Cricketers* p 137
[279] Webber *Chronicle of W G* p 84
[280] Sir Pelham Warner *Gentlemen v Players 1806-1949* p 148
[281] *Wisden* 1875 p 119
[282] E W Swanton *Daily Telegraph* 18 July 1998
[283] Webber *The Chronicle of W G* p 1083

Dr Midwinter refers. Although from not dissimilar social backgrounds, the two men went off in different directions, Grace to become perhaps the best-known Victorian, apart from the Queen herself and possibly Gladstone, and Pooley via professional cricket to the workhouse. Each of the two men had a respect for the other's cricketing ability. Pooley was the elder by six years. His death coincided with W G's fifty-ninth birthday. His obituary in *Licensing World* confirms Pooley's view of Grace along with a nice little anecdote:

In Pooley's opinion and that of his contemporaries there will never be another cricketer like W G Grace, who was once playing in Hertfordshire under an assumed name, and had scored over a century, when Ted Pooley unexpectedly appeared on the scene and disclosed "W G's" real identity[284]

It's a nice story, but scarcely believable. Why should W G Grace be playing under an assumed name? And how could such a well known national figure conceal his identity? What on earth did he do with his beard? According to J R Webber's meticulously researched chronicle, W G played five minor matches in Hertfordshire. In only one did he score a century - at Buntingford on 30 April 1875 (other versions say 20 or 29 April). As the team involved was *W G Grace's XI*, it is hardly credible that the captain would have sought to conceal his identity.[285]

Their first on-the-field encounter verged on the farcical. It was in the Gentlemen v Players match at Lord's in 1866, W G bowling to Pooley.

In his next over Pooley slogged one to the off up the hill past the scoring box and it lodged among some sacks in a shed close behind; it should have counted as a 4, but to all intents and purposes it was a lost ball; " on the sack; on the sack" cried a dozen voices and the enlightened fielder spotted the ball and threw it in and four were run.[286]

Nor were such semi-farcical incidents restricted to matches when Pooley and W G opposed each other. Three years later they were batting together for the South against the North at Bramall Lane when

---

[284]. 27 July 1907
[285] Webber *The Chronicle of W G* p192
[286]   Ib p 51

Pooley went for a second run and was right in W G's crease, and he would undoubtedly have been run out but Wootton shied at the wicket and Plumb was unable to handle the ball. [287]

With two colourful characters such as Pooley and W G Grace on opposite sides as they were in the earliest Surrey-Gloucestershire clashes, controversy and acrimony were never going to be far away. In the first official match between the two counties in 1870, Gloucestershire fielded an all amateur team at Durdham Down. It was the only first-class fixture ever staged there and the boundary was marked by a series of flags with the result that the outfield was encroached upon by eager spectators.

In W G's next over Pooley hit his first ball to long-leg for 2 then sent the last ball of the over on to the ladies' tent at square leg, taking the score to 7 in twenty-five minutes. In W G's next over Pooley drove a ball to the on where it was stopped by the spectators who were closely packed in the outfield and 4 were scored; Pooley said he would not continue batting until they were moved further out. Eventually they did go, but it enabled Filgate at long-leg to go further out and, two balls later Pooley hit one up to a tremendous height in his direction and it was well judged and brilliantly caught.[288]

Pooley was at his peak as a batsman in the early seventies and scored useful runs against all-comers, including Gloucestershire, but the atmosphere was distinctly soured in 1875 when, as wicket-keeper, he became involved in yet another controversial incident at Bristol.

Bush was given run out; he moved out of his crease after making his ground and the ball was thrown to Southerton [sic - contemporary accounts say Pooley] who put down the wicket; W G came on to the field and spoke to the Surrey fieldsmen; contemporary opinion was not impressed by this.[289]

A most unseemly disturbance followed, play was stopped, and a member of the Grace family not playing made himself very conspicuous. If such men as this question a perfectly correct decision of an umpire, we cannot help thinking the game must suffer. [Bell's Life]

A most unpleasant incident took place towards the end of the first day's play. Pooley made an appeal for run out against R E Bush. Mortlock gave it out. The batsman retired rather reluctantly, and immediately some of the spectators cried 'Not out'. W G now made his appearance and went into the field talking to the

---

287   Ib p 90
288   Ib p 98
289   Ib p 210

Surrey fieldsmen. Some most hideous noises were made by a few of the spectators. [The Field]

At 33 the ball had just been returned whilst a run was made; both men got in their ground, but Mr Bush stepped over the crease and was standing outside, when Pooley signalled to Street to shy the ball down. He did so, and Pooley put the wicket down and on appeal the Surrey umpire [Mortlock] decided that Mr Bush was run out. The affair gave rise to considerable dispute, and a great deal of angry contention, it being alleged that the ball was out of play at the time.

That was *Wisden* quoting *The Sportsman*. The Almanack then takes the high moral ground:

It is deplorable that cricketers and spectators frequently ignore the fact that Rule XXXVI explicitly states - "The Umpires are the sole judges of fair and unfair play, and *all disputes shall be determined by them.*" Play was stopped for a while by this "incident"

Nonetheless, W G, professional in all but name had a great respect for the professionalism of his regular opponent and in his *Cricket* under 'Cricketers I have met'' wrote admiringly of his keeping to slow bowling, his batting and his approach to the game (See Appendix C2).[290]

As is clear from contemporary evidence, some but, as we have seen in the Bush incident, by no means all, anecdotal, W G was no lover of umpires. Unlike many, however, Pooley was not, during his occasional appearances as an umpire, overwhelmed by W G's temperament or reputation.

At times, Dr W G had a penchant for remaining at the wicket after being given out. Pooley, the old Surrey wicket-keeper, being umpire at the bowler's end, gave him, l.b.w. Not being satisfied, Dr W G ran to the umpire saying 'Which leg did it hit, Pooley, which leg did it hit?' Pooley replied: 'Never mind which leg it hit; I've given you out and out you've got to go.'[291]

It is one of several variations on Grace-Pooley anecdotes. Most are probably apocryphal, but they are, nevertheless, in keeping with what is known of the characters of the two men. One version of "The crowd have come to see me bat, not to see you umpire" is associated with Pooley and

---

[290] W G Grace *Cricket* p 359-60
[291] *Memorial Biography* p 169

there is a good yarn about Pooley placing an upturned spiked boot in the doctor's bed. [292]

If twentieth-century cricketers sometimes complain from the comfort of their sponsored cars of too much travelling and too much cricket, then perhaps they should take time out occasionally to look at the amount of cricket played in the mid-nineteenth century. Above the surface are the 'grand' or 'important' matches, but below those, the remainder of the iceberg comprises a bewildering mixture of matches against the odds, single wicket encounters, 'pros' as 'given men' as the game's journeymen do their best to maximise their earnings by playing as much cricket as possible and hoping for a benefit. Early in his career, Pooley played as a private professional in Perth and Northern Ireland and he had many other appearances as a "given man". To take a completely random sample, at various times and in various places, he also appeared for Twenty-two of the Middlesex Club, with Pooley and Silcock;[293] Pooley, Bennett and Humphrey v Wootton, Pryor and Lillywhite;[294] Southgate with Pooley v Surrey Club with Caesar[295], Twenty-two of Edinburgh with Atkinson, W McIntyre and Pooley v All England Eleven[296] Four of the South v Four of the North on the Race Course at Northampton[297] Fifteen Surrey Colts with Pooley v Surrey Club [298], Sixteen Players of Richmond and District with R Humphrey and E Pooley v Richmond Club with W G Grace[299] etc, etc....But it was quantity rather than quality. And professional cricketers did not grow fat in the proceeds. Quite the contrary. In his *Old Ebor* interview, Pooley recollects playing at Edinburgh with the USEE. On their return, he and Mortlock had 1s 4d between them[300]. The details may, as in the remainder of this interview, be exaggerated or minimised for dramatic effect, but the reality was that most professional cricketers, during their career and certainly after it, had a constant struggle to make ends meet and it was not only Edward Pooley who was to end his life in great poverty. So did Jupp and the two Humphreys, Richard by his own hand: so did Julius Caesar and many others.

---

[292] Douglas Fairey *Weekend - How Amazing Grace gave Umpires the Boot* April 12-18 1978
[293] *S & B* Vol VIII p 205
[294]   Ib   p 510
[295]   Ib   Vol IX p 72
[296]   Ib   Vol XI p 28
[297]   Ib   Vol XII p 592
[298]   Ib   Vol XIII p 26
[299]   Ib   p 757
[300] Pullin *Talks with Old English Cricketers* p 139

CHAPTER 11

HOW GOOD WAS HE? - POOLEY, THE CRICKETER; POOLEY, THE MAN

Like most wicket-keepers, a small man, Pooley stood no more than 5ft 6in. At his best he weighed 9st, but towards the end of his career, 10st 6 or 11 stone[301]

How good was he? It is unrealistic to apply the standards of the twentieth-century to the nineteenth when pitches were different, overarm bowling not universal and the approach to wicket-keeping was to stand up to everything and use a long-stop. So a 'c Pooley b Southerton' entry can be compared with a 'c Pinder b Freeman', but not realistically with 'c Marsh b Lillee' or 'c Stewart b Gough'.

In 1889, *The Badminton Library of Sports and Pastimes* had attempted to analyse the art of wicket-keeping and to assess the relative qualities of its recent practitioners.

A player with no aptitude for wicket-keeping on first going to that position will undergo moments of unspeakable agony. Spectators do not generally realise the position of the wicket-keeper, indeed nobody can who has not attempted the art. In the first place we will suppose a very fast bowler; in the second a fast and possibly rather bumpy wicket; in the third place a batsman with the bulk of W G Grace or Roger Iddison, wielding a bat of unorthodox proportions; and in the fourth place, three stumps with two bails placed on the top. The body of the batsman in many cases completely obstructs the view the wicket-keeper ought to have of the ball. Even if he can get a good sight of the ball there is that abominable bat being fiddled about baulking the eyesight in the most tantalising manner, and there are some batsmen who have a provoking habit of waving their bats directly the bowler begins his run, and continuing their antics till the ball is right up to them. The wicket-keeper is grimly told that he must not flinch, and that he can never be really good if he does not keep his legs still. True, most true; but like other great people who do great things, he must resist every natural impulse and all his lower nature, and not till he has succeeded will he stand the least chance of reaching to a pinnacle of excellence. Having briefly pointed the difficulties and dangers, let us beg the field to treat the wicket-keeper as tenderly as possible, to cultivate a straight throw, either a catch or a long-hop, and not

---

[301] *S & B* Vol VIII p 430

half-volleys or, worse still, short-hops, and never to throw hard when there is no necessity. If the throw is crooked, the wicket-keeper should not leave his position to stop it; leave that to the men who are backing up. He may be called upon afterwards to put down the wicket, and he ought to be in a position for so doing. Bear in mind also this cardinal rule - namely, to stand behind the wicket to a throw and not in front....

The greatest wicket-keepers since 1860 in England have been Lockyer, Pooley, Pilling and Pinder, and we ask Plumb and Sherwin to forgive us. To discriminate between the first four is impossible; we merely remark that to the genuine slows of the pace of Southerton and Peate, we reckon Pooley to have been the best that ever lived, and to the very fast, Pinder at his prime was unequalled. Still Pooley was not so good to fast, nor Pinder to slow; and on the whole we think the four may be put on an equality. [302]

Of Pooley's 854 first-class dismissals, 358 were stumped. At almost 42%, that represents a higher proportion than any contemporary or subsequent wicket-keeper. Up to the Second World War, the proportion was usually between 20 - 30% and for current 'keepers the highest figures are 10-12%. It is not sought to demonstrate from these figures that Pooley was four times better than his successors, but simply to illustrate the way in which the art of wicket-keeping has changed over the years.

Pooley played in 370 first-class matches and, given that there were a dozen or so matches in the early sixties and subsequent occasions on which he played, but injury prevented him from keeping, he averaged one stumping per match which statistically puts him way ahead of anyone else in the history of the game. Les Ames, who holds the world record 418 took 593 matches to do it (about 0.7 per match) and Steven Rhodes has the highest rate among contemporary glove-men with about 0.33 - again demonstrating the way in which the game has changed. Of Pooley's contemporaries, Phillips had 195 in 216 (0.9), Pilling 206 in 250 (0.82), Pinder 137 in 179 (0.77) and Plumb 15 in 26 (0.58).

Contemporary opinion was that his keeping to slow bowling was unsurpassed, but was less convinced about his ability to keep to fast bowling. His obituary in *The Times* encapsulates the view that he was one of the finest wicket-keepers to play the game, but inferior to Pinder and

---

[302] p 278

Plumb to very fast bowling. It does go on to point out that his opportunities of keeping to pace bowlers were restricted. [303]

Haygarth's compliments are also not without qualification. Throughout *Scores and Biographies* and in the Pooley pen-portrait in particular, he is at pains to emphasise that Pooley's success owed much to the slow pace of the Oval pitch and the proportion of his wickets taken from Southerton's "tempting insinuators". [304]

It was not a point of view with which Pooley would have concurred - or at least admitted publicly. He paid Pinder the compliment of saying he was the smartest at taking a ball that he saw, but that he did not always look for the "psychological moment" when the batsman had his foot off the crease. He reminds any critics that he, Pooley, has kept to Freeman and Tarrant, "two of the fastest bowlers in England". [305]

It was, however, as wicket-keeper to Southerton that Pooley was at his absolute peak. Of his 375 catches and 250 stumpings for Surrey in 256 matches 127, all but one as wicket-keeper, and 148 respectively were from Southerton, who had played for Surrey as early as 1854 and 1855, but not bowled. From 1867, however,

Southerton began the long period of his career as a successful bowler, which joins his name to those of Jupp, Humphrey and Pooley as the greatest in Surrey cricket for the next decade. [306]

Thus, almost half his total dismissals and almost 60% of his stumpings were captured in conjunction with the round-arm off-spinner.

Although Pooley was succeeded as Surrey's wicket-keeper by an amateur in the shape of W W Read, at the time when he was at his peak, the job was very much the province of the professional.

Thirty years ago the professional wicket-keeper was a class, even two classes above the amateur. Lockyer, Pooley, Plumb, and Pinder formed a class that the amateurs could not show any comparison with. Possibly the rougher wickets

---

[303] *Times* 19 July 1907
[304] . *S & B* Vol VIII p 430
[305] Pullin *Talks with Old English Cricketers* p141
[306] Alverstone & Alcock *Surrey Cricket* pp 82-3

and the, generally speaking, faster bowling made the position more unpleasant than it is now, but undoubtedly the amateur has improved beyond all knowledge in wicket-keeping and there is not much to choose now.[307]

F S Ashley-Cooper, editing Rev James Pycroft's classic *The Cricket Field* takes a similar line

At wicket-keeping, the men of labour ought to beat the men of leisure. Hard hands are essential and hard hands can only come from hard work...
But Pooley's name stands the highest of all; the certainty and facility with which he takes all kinds of bowling, both with the right hand and the left can hardly be surpassed....
The great thing in wicket-keeping is for hand and eye to go together, just as with batting, and what is exercise for the former assists the latter. Any exercise in which the hand habitually tries to obey the eye, is useful for Cricket, fielding improves batting, and batting improves fielding. The sixteen principal wicket-keepers of the last fifty years were all efficient batsmen.[308]

The Times said he was quite first-rate as a batsman and he would have made many more runs if he had not so often suffered from damaged hands.[309]

Richard Daft in his *Kings of Cricket* admires Pooley's batting, but is not slow to detect a flaw.

Pooley was a worthy successor of the great Tom Lockyer as a wicket-keeper, and was also a very good bat indeed. He had a very hard hit on the off-side [sic] to mid-wicket, but was often caught out in that place. When I fielded there I stood a few yards further back for him than I ever did for anyone else, and have caught him out more than once.[310]

Pooley's attitude on the field was hard and what in modern terms would be called professional. We have seen how, over the years, he was involved in a number of incidents - the Absolom 'obstructing the field' in 1868, the Nepean run out in 1870, the Charlwood 'hit the ball twice' in 1872, the appeal against W G Grace for obstructing the field in 1874 and the Bush run out in 1875, which some might see as contravening the spirit of the game. *Bailey's Magazine*, referring to Pooley's record 12 dismissals in a match says:

---

[307] Horace G Hutchinson (Ed) *Country Life Library of Sports - Cricket* p 213-4
[308] pp 256-8
[309] 19 July 1907
[310] *Anecdotes and Reminiscences 1858 to 1892*

The wicket-keeping of Pooley has been something marvellous, and we do not believe that even Lockyer in his best time was equal to him. It is to be regretted that being so good he should persist in the absurd tricks which bring him applause at The Oval. [311]

What these absurd tricks are is not defined, but there may be a clue in Pooley's observation in the Old Ebor interview that Pinder failed to look for the psychological moment when the batsman's heel was lifted from the line. Additionally, there is a strong hint in the text accompanying a reproduction of the 1871 Ordnance Survey map of Kennington and Walworth, held in the Guildhall Library, which, dealing with The Oval and those who had trod its turf has this to say :

The Oval had a less class conscious air than Lords, and was a ground where a boisterous shout with its echo is not regarded as a breach of etiquette, and a little homely badinage is not construed into vulgarity....
Edward Pooley was a proud figure then, who won many stumpings by pretending the ball had passed him by, but few batsmen will have wished for his gloomy end. Twenty years of wicket-keeping so damaged his hands that he was unfit for any other work, and in his enforced retirement he remained a familiar but sadder sight at the Oval, coming back to beg for support. He was forced to seek shelter at the local workhouse. Cricket was always a hard game.

Part of the truth certainly, but by no means all of it.

In reviewing the years between 1865 and 1875, the brochure celebrating Surrey's 150th Anniversary refers to the emergence of "Ted Pooley, who kept wicket no less than 256 times for Surrey" (Actually, he didn't: he made 256 appearances, but did not keep wicket in every match, particularly in the early part of his career).

Erratic of temper and demeanour, readers should refer to his beguiling yet sorrowful life-story when they hear some drab modern described as a 'character'. [312]

Leaving aside whether it is Pooley or the readers who might be erratic of temper and demeanour, we have already mentioned the reference in his *Wisden* Obituary to faults of private character that marred Pooley's career

---

[311] quoted in Lemmon *The History of Surrey County Cricket Club* p 39
[312] *Surrey County Cricket Club: 150 Years: A Celebration* p41

and were the cause of the poverty in which he spent the later years of his life.[313]

Gambling seems to have been the principal one of the faults and there seems no other explanation for the disappearance of a reasonable benefit, grants from the Club and pay from odd jobs, his decline to abject poverty and a choice of "the workhouse or the river".[314] Although he was a long way from being an abstainer, there is no evidence that drink was a problem for him. His association with the Albany beer house in Richmond, however, brought him into contact with the licensed trade and its *habitués,* Southerton's comments on the Pooley anatomy suggest a high capacity for alcohol and the provenance on one of his admissions to the workhouse is recorded as the Duchy of Cornwall Public House, Bowling Green Street. So, there may not have been alcohol-addiction, but his fondness for and association with it could not have helped. If one were to name the social vices of the nineteenth century, there is at least a likelihood that among them would be tobacco, alcohol, gambling and womanising. To a greater or lesser extent, this outstanding cricketer had them all.

He was a man's man, with perhaps an element of the loveable rogue. Despite his large family, he does not seem to have many characteristics of what in the twentieth century would be described as a family man. He certainly lost touch with his extensive family and the evidence is that this was not accidental, but a conscious move on their part to dissociate themselves from him He may have remained in touch with his brother Frederick with whom he had played in 1876 and 1877. His father had died in 1880 and his widowed mother just after the end of his playing career in 1884.

He recognised the social order (in reality, before the First World war there was little opportunity not to), but social superiority was not synonymous with moral superiority and though he called the amateurs, his superiors 'Sir' or 'Mr', he in no way accepted that their judgments on cricketing matters might be better than his own.

---

[313] *Wisden* 1908 pp 147-9
[314] Pullin *Talks with Old English Cricketers* p 131

Surrey committee member, Frederick Gale tells a story[315] of Pooley's reaction to the Surrey début in 1871 of William Game, then aged 17 and at Sherborne School, later to gain a blue in all four of his years at Oxford. It is an instructive tale in that it illustrates simultaneously Pooley's short fuse, his acknowledgement of the social order, his belief in his own judgment and his respect for the ability of a fellow-cricketer, be he amateur or professional.

In the evening of the first day of the match [against Yorkshire at The Oval] I happened to get in the same railway carriage as Pooley, and I asked him what he thought of Game. He said, "I was very wild in the morning, sir. There was a letter from Mr Burrup saying 'Mr Game is to play and Mr Gale says he is to go to long-leg.' I said to myself, 'Oh, Mr Gale is to captain the whole team then, I suppose.' After a short time, one of the Yorkshiremen made a long hit, which Mr Game went for, and from a distance of ninety yards the ball dropped hard into my hands. As I was walking across after the over I said to him, 'Can you generally throw like that, sir?' [note the 'Mr' and 'Sir', though Pooley was 29 and Game 17] Oh, yes, he replied. So I told him not to be afraid to throw in hard at me and well - look at my hands now, sir! He has punished me all day but his fielding was so brilliant that if that young gent played for All England, and never had an innings at all, he would be worth a man and a-half to his side"

It was, incidentally, Frederick Gale who, two years later, was to propose Pooley's reinstatement after his suspension because of the Sheffield incident and with William Game in 1882 that Pooley was to share a partnership of 89 on his way to his final first-class 50. One is reminded of Trevelyan's dictum that if the French noblesse had been capable of playing cricket with their peasants, their chateaux would never have been burnt[316]

Genial and extrovert, Pooley remained, despite his short fuse, a sociable character, popular on the field and off it who, even in the dark days of his decline had his admirers and supporters, who, recalling happier days, were prepared to do what little they could for him.

His Obituary in *The Times*, even allowing for a *de mortuis, nil nisi bonum* ethos, is categorical that no one who follows the game at all closely will need to be told that in his day he was one of the most popular of the Surrey players and Old Ebor comments that "the same jaunty mien and airy cheerfulness" have survived Pooley's other misfortunes. Likewise, his

---

[315] Bettesworth *Chats on the Cricket Field* p 446
[316] *English Social History* Ch 8

obituary in *Licensing World* points to his popularity as a player and later resilience during his illness.

Pooley was not a modest man and embellished the incidents and accidents of his career with bravado. Jem Mace, the prize fighter is alleged to have said the he would rather face any man in England for an hour than keep wicket for five minutes and Pooley dismissed as "nothing" losing three teeth at Lord's and having his nose broken in Jersey.[317]

Wicket-keeping and rheumatism had taken their toll on his hands. He spent some time in the Royal Mineral Water Hospital at Bath[318], the Charing Cross Hospital and the Marylebone Infirmary[319]. Every finger and both thumbs had at some stage been broken and, says Old Ebor, the joints were knotted and gnarled in a way which suggested the thumbscrew rather than the wicket-keeper's gloves.[320]

In his failure to adjust to life after cricket he was not alone. There are numerous parallel examples in his own generation and in earlier and later ones. But, although he was not treated ungenerously by the Club in financial terms, the support systems that were to characterise the twentieth century were not yet in place. Reminiscing over past times and how much easier life is nowadays, both on and off the field. are not peculiar to Pooley and his generation, but it is a sad fact that *La recherche du Temps Perdu*, with all its futile implications took precedence over adjusting to the present.

---

[317] Pullin *Talks with Old English Cricketers* pp 134-5
[318] Roger Packham *The Troubles of Edward Pooley*
[319] Pullin *Talks with Old English Cricketers* pp 131
[320] Ib   p 134

CHAPTER 12

THE WANDERING OUTLAW: DECLINE AND FALL (1884/1907)

The wandering outlaw of his own dark mind
BYRON. Childe Harold's Pilgrimage

Between his retirement from professional cricket in 1883 and his first admission to the Renfrew Road Workhouse in Lambeth in 1898, Edward Pooley had a number of disjointed appointments. In 1881 when he did not play a full season, Pooley, along with Richard Humphrey, Thomas's younger brother, had been engaged as scorer for three matches.[321] By the end of 1883, he was applying for an umpiring job for the following season but, as Jupp and Street were already in possession of the two available appointments, the application was, in the unemotional prose of the minutes "not entertained".[322] By March 1885, he was soliciting for employment and the Committee giving an assurance that it would be considered if an opening occurred.

He managed the occasional umpiring appointment with Surrey, though, unlike Street, Barratt and Jupp, was unable to command a regular contract and had a variety of other jobs, such as Manager of a billiard saloon at The Railway Hotel, Clapham; Groundkeeper and bowler to Strawberry Hill Cricket Club, Twickenham and Timekeeper at a Richmond building site[323]. In the 1891 Census, he describes himself as a Gardener, having appeared on Rose's birth certificate as a shorthand-writer. Given the state of his hands, that seems highly unlikely.

Sir Home Gordon wrote in the *Badminton Magazine*:

to see him in shabby clothes, with grizzly-white hair, and a strained, sordid appearance gazing at The Oval on the scene of his former triumphs, was pitiable.[324]

---

[321] SCCC mins 21 July 1881 SCRO 2042/1/4
[322] Ib   18 December 1883
[323] Packham *The Troubles of Edward Pooley*
[324] quoted in Sissons *The Players* p 149

In 1883, shortly after his benefit, Pooley is recorded in *Lillywhite's Cricketer's Companion* as residing at Fairfield Cottage, Hampton Wick; but by the end of the year he was soliciting for work as an umpire and two years later for any work at all. Various grants and allowances were paid to him over an extended period, but the Surrey Committee finally lost patience and discontinued them at the end of 1894. There were various subsequent pleas.

The family were living in Fulwell Road, Teddington in 1888[325]. In 1890 they were at 19 Barton Cottages, Twickenham[326], probably the same address as the 19 Denmark Road where Edward, Minnie and seven children were resident for the 1891 Census. Florence had still to be born and Ellen and Fanny had now disappeared from the scene. At this stage they would have been in their twenties and it is probable that they had left home and were now married. 19 Denmark Road today is a modern house, eleven years old, on a site previously occupied by garages. Until this point, the family had lived in respectable middle-class/skilled working-class areas. Fulwell Road in particular is a series of separate terraces, dated between 1880 and 1884, so it was new housing at the time they lived there. By the middle 1890s, however, the likelihood is that he had lost touch with his family and, in the later degeneration into poverty, he detached himself from them and they from him. Referring to his decision to seek the shelter of the workhouse, Pooley points to a disinclination to sponge on his friends or become a burden to his relatives. The likelihood is that it was no longer an option.[327] Indeed, anecdotal evidence in the family is that he was paid to go away... which he seems to have done and for a while the family was known by the mother's surname of Sabine. Meanwhile, Edward declined into ill-health and poverty, from the middle-classes to a workingmen's hostel and a penniless death in the workhouse.

..in the years prior to the First World War, with its dominant laissez-faire attitude, and in the absence of the welfare provisions which can now be taken for granted, formerly great professionals such as Pooley, could end their lives in desperate circumstances. Clubs such as Surrey, which made their wealth through the drawing power of players such as Pooley, have to accept some of the responsibility.[328]

---

[325] Birth certificate of Alfred Ernest, 6th child and 5th son by Minnie Sabine
[326] Birth certificate of Rose Emily, 7th child and 2nd daughter by Minnie Sabine
[327] Pullin *Talks with Old English Cricketers* p 131
[328] Sissons *The Players* p151

Possibly so, but there are limits and by 1894 the Committee clearly felt that those limits had been reached. In 1889, it had been resolved that a weekly grant of ten shillings be made to Pooley until 1 May.[329] It was, however, contingent on his good behaviour.

An umpiring vacancy was available later that year on the death of Henry Jupp in April, but it went to Barratt not to Pooley. A year later an application for further assistance was not granted[330], but by the Autumn, reports on Pooley's medical condition were being sought;[331] in December, his grant increased to 15s per week paid to him via the Revd Bayfield Clark,[332] who was presumably taking some responsibility for his moral welfare.

Shortly afterwards, the Committee's attention was drawn to an article in *The Sportsman* about Pooley's condition and the Secretary asked to point out that the former wicket-keeper had been in receipt of an allowance from the club for the last three winters. Reports were received on Pooley's condition, he attended the Committee and it was agreed to continue his grant for the time being [333]. By the end of 1894, however, the grants to Pooley and Humphrey were discontinued, an appeal from the two men cutting no ice with the Committee.[334]

It was also in 1894 or shortly afterwards that the rift with the family seems to have been complete. Since his retirement from the game, three more children had been born and, unlike their elder siblings, registered in the name of Pooley. They were Charles Victor (1884), Alfred Ernest (1888), and Rose Emily (1890). The youngest, Florence Annie, followed in 1894, by which time everyone, including doubtless Minnie, now approaching 40 and describing herself on birth certificates as "Pooley, formerly Sabine", had had enough. It may well be that the stigma of their illegitimacy had been kept from the family and perhaps only discovered when they wished to marry and needed to acquire a birth certificate. Alice married William

[329]	Ib	17 January 1889 SCRO 2042/1/5
[330]	Ib	20 March 1890
[331]	Ib	23 October and 20 November 1890
[332].	Ib	18 December 1890
[333]	Ib	7 May, 21 May, 16 July, 6 August 1891
[334]	Ib	18 November 1894

Arthur Morris at Brentford on 11 April 1896[335]. Although the marriage certificate records the bride's father's 'rank or profession' as 'professional cricketer', his name appears as 'Edward Sabine' - fairly powerful evidence that not only was Edward absent from his daughter's wedding, but that she was so ashamed of him that she was prepared to lie to the Registrar about his name in order to conceal the stigma of her illegitimacy. While the evidence is not absolutely conclusive, it is certainly a strong indication of a family rift and consonant with family memories of Edward's being paid to go. The grants from Surrey had been discontinued and the family were probably in a position to pay. In 1904, Alice and her husband were witnesses of the wedding of John Harold[336]. After her estrangement from Edward, Minnie, now in her late forties, continued to attract admirers, principal among whom, according to family recollections, was a Mr Stuckey. By this time, however, Edward was off the family scene and a virtually permanent inmate of the Lambeth Workhouse. The gradual decline in health and self-respect which originated towards the end of his playing days now began to accelerate sharply.

Richard Humphrey continued in poor circumstances and eventually drowned himself in the Thames in 1906. From 1898, Pooley was in and out of the workhouse, but through the columns of the *Sportsman* and the officers of the Royal Exchange Assurance, he continued to solicit for employment, pensions and grants.[337]

"For the poor always ye have with you" we are reminded in St John's gospel. It is a truism and a social problem that different societies at different times have attempted to solve in different ways. The first Poor Laws of England date from 1601 and saw a number of amendments and refinements until 1834 when Lord Althorp, later the third Earl Spencer, but then Chancellor of the Exchequer, was instrumental in getting on to the Statute Book the Poor Law (Amendment) Act which saw the workhouse become a gloomy, but integral part of the Victorian social scene. Introduced as a measure to replace the parish-based Speenhamland system, presented as a humanitarian measure and receiving cross-party support, the main motivation behind the Act was economic, the costs of poor relief

---

[335] Alice Minnie's marriage certificate
[336] John Harold's marriage cerificate
[337]   Ib   20 October 1898, 15 March 1900, 17 April 1902

129

having escalated in the wake of the industrial revolution and spawned abuses which saw the unemployed and low-paid subsidised from the rates.

Historically, the role of personal responsibility in relation to welfare benefits has been the subject of more or less continuous debate during the last two centuries. The creation of a national workhouse system after 1834 was designed to reassert the importance of individual effort by fit adults, and to cut back on what was seen as over-generous public provision of welfare benefits to them. [338]

The object of the new system was to provide shelter for those without it and work for those capable of it, an example of the current welfare to work ethos in fact. In its attempts to distinguish between the "deserving poor" and the less deserving, it reflected the Victorian penchant for classification and categorisation and the prison, the lunatic asylum and the workhouse form a trio of institutions, which made for administrative tidiness, but caused untold misery for those who, for whatever reason, were confined within their gloomy and forbidding walls. The workhouse system survived until after the first World War and the 1834 Poor Law was not finally repealed until 1948.

The fear of the workhouse with its degrading conditions was one of the most potent for the infirm and elderly poor in the 19th century, and the dismantling of the workhouse system and the introduction of old age pensions in the first decades of the 20th century was greeted with near-universal relief. The old, frequently solid - if grim - workhouse buildings in towns were commonly turned into hospitals; many still survive. [339]

"It is Christmas Day in the Workhouse" is, like "The boy stood on the burning deck", one of those poems of which everyone can (mis)quote the first line, but of which few know the sequel. It is one of the most parodied poems in the English language, but the subsequent lines of George R Sims paint a picture of less than benevolent despotism.

It was to one of 600 or so such institutions, the Renfrew Road Workhouse in Lambeth, built in 1871 to accommodate 1221 (What superb Victorian precision!) men, women and children - though numbers were rarely below

---

[338] Anne Digby *British Welfare Policy: Workhouse to Workfare* p6
[339] *The History Today Companion to British History* p825

1400[340] - that Edward Pooley presented himself on 12 December 1898, having been faced with the choice of "the workhouse or the river". [341]

The Lambeth Board of Guardians controlled both the Workhouse and the Lambeth Infirmary which were amalgamated in 1922 under the new name of Lambeth Hospital.

The segregation arrangements reflected the intention of the Poor Law Amendment Act.

Each class has its own and distinct day-room, dormitories, staircases. lavatories, waterclosets, airing ground and workrooms; the only common place of meeting being the chapel and dining-room, where conversational intercourse is forbidden. The several classes in each sex are for aged, able-bodied of good character, and two subdivisions of able-bodied of bad character. [342]

Resident in the same workhouse earlier in the year were a nine year old Charlie Chaplin, his mother and half-brother Sidney. It was the first of several visits. It is whimsical to speculate whether the paths of the holder of a world wicket-keeping record and the future world-famous star of the silent screen may have crossed. Because of the very strict segregation by age, sex and character it is highly unlikely. The "idle and profligate" were accommodated at the coldest end of dormitories, while the "infirm and guiltless" or elderly had slightly less inhospitable conditions; but there was perhaps sufficient difference for Pooley to be motivated to add four years to his age at this point, hoping to qualify for the "infirm and guiltless" category and saving the master the decision as to whether to categorise him as good, bad or very bad character. At the turn of the century, 60 would be regarded as elderly. Only 1% of the population was over 65, compared with 8% in the 1990s and a projected 20% by 2020.

Work, which Pooley probably managed to avoid on health grounds, was kept as boring as possible to discourage applications for admission and included bone-breaking, stone-breaking and untwining rope for re-use in caulking ship's timbers. Diet was potatoes, cabbage, tea and gruel. Susannah Smith, architectural historian and archivist, researching the history of Greet House, a similar institution in Nottinghamshire has

---

[340] *Lambeth Hospital Fifty Years Retrospect* in Minet Library, London Borough of Lambeth
[341] Pullin *Talks with Old English Cricketers* p 131
[342] *The Builder* January 24 1874

identified "a pervading sense of isolation..combined with a lack of privacy. There were no freedoms. There was endless boredom."[343]

On his first acquaintance with the institution, Pooley stayed 19 days and was out on New Year's Eve. But by the following winter a recurrence of rheumatism forced him back to the bleak institution in Renfrew Road. When admitted a year earlier, his provenance was given as Rowton House, Bond Street. Now, on 31 October 1899, he is recorded as having "no home".[344] The Rowton Houses, of which the one in Bond Street, Vauxhall where Pooley resided before his first admission to the workhouse was the first, were the brainchild of Montagu Williams Lowry, Lord Rowton, who had been Private Secretary to Disraeli and helped to set up the Guinness Trust in 1890. They were working men's hostels, designed to provide for 6d a night clean sheets, tiled wash rooms, foot-baths, washing troughs for clothes, hot water and a lodgers' kitchen so that residents could cook their own food - conditions which, while not designed to be luxurious, were manifestly superior to those which obtained in the workhouse.[345] The Vauxhall Rowton House eventually became part of the Rowton Hotels Group and as the Centrepoint Vauxhall Hostel and Job Club has now reverted to something fairly close to its original function.

From here Pooley had arrived for his first brief period in the workhouse and presumably returned there on his discharge. Ten months later, however, his domestic circumstances were clearly less favourable and doubtless contributed to a longer stay, this time for the whole of the winter and most of the following Spring. He was discharged at his own request on 25 May 1900, having in the meantime been in touch with the Surrey committee. At a meeting on 15 March, an application for employment was "not entertained".[346]

Within two weeks, he was back. Again, the "From whence admitted" column in the Creed Register reads "Rowton House", So Pooley had found his way back there or was lying!

---

343 Caroline McGhie *A Bright future at the Workhouse* Sunday Telegraph October 11, 1998
344 Creed Registers of Renfrew Road Workhouse, Lambeth
345 *The London Encyclopædia* ed Ben Weinreb and Christopher Hibbert
346 Surrey C C C minutes (Surrey County Record Office 2042/1/6)

His stay this time was over a year, from 8 June 1900 to 1 August 1901. He now made attempts to secure himself a pension. In April 1902, the Surrey Committee was approached by one A A Percival of the Royal Exchange Assurance with the suggestion of a pension for Pooley. The facts in Percival's letter were apparently not correct, but the Committee nevertheless agreed to consider the case and referred the matter to the Finance Committee. A month later, the final crunch came with the following resolution:

After carefully considering the application of Mr A A Percival [Royal Exchange Assurance] re Pooley and seeing what the Committee had done for him since 1884 the Committee do not see their way to make any further grant to him. [347]

Pooley then approached the President of the Club, but at its meeting on 5 June, the Committee confirmed its earlier resolution.[348] After more than a year out of the workhouse, he returned, again from Rowton House, on 30 December 1902.

On 27 February 1903 Pooley was one of 35 inmates transferred to the Risbridge Union in Suffolk as part of national workhouse policy. His quest for funds from the club continued and, in December, a letter from him was read to the Committee, asking for help with his subscription to the Cricketers Fund (Why, at this time of his life, is Pooley, now claiming to be 65, but actually just past his 61st birthday, making contributions *to* the Fund?). It was resolved, that part of his subscription having been paid, the Committee remit the balance to the Secretary of the Cricketers Fund Friendly Society. It was his last communication with the Committee. [349]

He was returned to Lambeth on 30 July 1904 and discharged himself the same day. After only two months he was back for the sixth and last time, this time admitted from the Duchy of Cornwall Public House in Bowling Green Street, an address also given on his death certificate, though whether he was actually resident at the said hostelry or just "passing through" is open to speculation. On 29 September 1906 he was discharged to the Infirmary where on the morning of Thursday 18 July 1907, he died of arterio-sclerosis, cardiac failure and a rodent ulcer. His great contemporary W G Grace was celebrating his fifty-ninth birthday, Hayward and Hobbs

---

[347] Ib
[348] Ib
[349] Ib

were opening the innings for Surrey against Lancashire at The Oval where the previous day - Pooley would have been pleased had he known - the Players had beaten the Gentlemen by 54 runs. Coincidentally, there was a meeting of the Surrey County Cricket Club Committee later the same day. It was resolved that the Club would meet his funeral expenses.

A hundred years on, it is not our place to condone or condemn, but simply to observe that while he may have been his own enemy, he was also perhaps a victim of circumstances who failed to escape from the triple influence of his family background, the world of professional cricket and the Victorian social scene.

The Workhouse is still there, the Master's quarters now occupied by the Ronald Grant Film Archive and part of the remainder converted to the Woodlands Nursing Home. The Brook Street (now Brook Drive) Infirmary is also still there, a small part of it used by the Lambeth Community Care Centre, but otherwise boarded up, derelict, desolate and deserted. Its eerily silent and neglected grounds are now used mainly as a shortcut from Brook Drive to Renfrew Road. Apart from traces of the occasional dosser there are few signs of life. It is more difficult to believe that the traffic chaos of the Elephant and Castle is but a few hundred yards away than to imagine the ghost of Edward Pooley stalking this lunar wilderness.

The Workhouse had a contract for burials with Lambeth Cemetery. The Superintendent's Register of Interments reduces the life and death of the poor to stark economics. The fee for a pauper's funeral, met by the parish, was 7/6, 1/6 for a stillborn child.[350] There is, however, no entry for Edward Pooley, nor is there any record of his being buried at either of the other two sites used at times of pressure (which, being high summer with no epidemics around, it wasn't) namely, the Streatham and South Metropolitan (West Norwood) Burial Grounds. An examination of the Lambeth cemetery, where the recollection of the family is that he was buried, has revealed nothing, but in a huge necropolis where even graves dating from the 1970s are neglected and overgrown, there was little hope of finding any trace of one whose neglect in death paralleled his own self-neglect in life.

As elusive in death as he was in life, he has no known grave.

---

[350] Minet Library, London Borough of Lambeth

APPENDIX A

POOLEY YEAR-BY-YEAR

Each year, the various Lillywhite Publications commented on the quality of the leading cricketers of the day. Amateurs and professionals were treated separately. Here is a selection of what they had to say about Pooley over his 23 seasons as a professional cricketer.

Guide to Cricketers

1861

Poolley [sic] Edward   A promising player for the county, by care and attention to his older colleagues. He bats well, and in good form, is an excellent field

1863

Pooley Edward   a player who with some little more steadiness, would no doubt appear more prominently in his county's scoring-book. He is a good field, an excellent bat, and takes long-leg first-rate

1864

One approaching, and very fast too, to be an "A1". A splendid wicket-keeper, beautiful bat, and a good change bowler, therefore, useful in any eleven. Plays for Surrey (born) and Middlesex (residence), on which ground he is engaged

1865

He is a cricketer all over, quite first rate as a wicket-keeper and bat - bar the dropping of his knee to cause a leg before wicket. Good anywhere in the field and an excellent change bowler

Cricketers' Companion

1864

He is a splendid wicket-keeper, treading hard on Lockyer's heels; has improved very much as a batsman and is a good bowler

1865-66

he is a splendid wicket-keeper; has improved very much as a batsman and is a good bowler

1867-77

splendid wicket-keeper; very fine batsman

1878-82

a splendid wicket-keeper and fine free batsman

1883

a splendid wicket-keeper and fine free batsman; did not play for Surrey after July, received a benefit last year

Cricketers' Annual

1871-78

The finest wicket-keeper of the day without doubt; a very effective batsman too with great powers of hitting, and can score from any bowling

1879

The finest wicket-keeper of the day without doubt; an effective batsman too with great powers of hitting, though not so successful of late.

1880

Still the finest wicket-keeper of the day, without doubt. An effective batsman too with great powers of hitting, and played some good innings towards the end of the season

1881-82

Fine wicket-keeper, an effective batsman too with great powers of hitting

1883

Fine wicket-keeper, an effective batsman too with great powers of hitting; had a benefit last year and has practically retired

APPENDIX B

ANNUAL STATISTICS (FIRST-CLASS)

Year	Matches	Inns	NO	HS	RUNS	Av'ge	100/50	O	M	R	W	Avge	BB	Ct/St
1861	2	3	1	15*	19	9.50	-/-							1/-
1862	8	12	3	17	75	8.33	-/-							2/-
1863	3	5	-	16	44	8.80	-/-							2/1
1864	11	16	2	36*	188	13.42	-/-							9/8
1865	17	29	3	82*	530	20.38	-/2	11	2	16	-	-	-	18/3
1866	15	26	2	49	349	14-54	-/-	53.3	6	152	3	50.66	2-39	17/10
1867	20	37	3	85	690	20.29	-/5							39/22
1868	23	41	1	51	584	14.60	-/3	18	2	54	-	-	-	42/39
1869	21	38	1	88	780	21.08	-/5	7	-	12	-	-	-	33/24
1870	27	52	5	94	1084	23.06	-/6	4	1	7	-	-	-	43/36
1871	22	40	1	125	926	23.74	1/4	2	1	7	-	-	-	23/14
1872	28	46	1	52	629	13.97	-/2							28/31
1873	6	12	-	19	96	8.00	-/-							8/7
1874	22	39	5	97	594	17.47	-/2	43	11	79	3	26.33	1-1	37/12
1875	22	41	3	32	462	12.15	-/-	14	-	47	-	-	-	38/23
1876	26	46	5	63	732	17.85	-/1	4	-	16	-	-	-	37/27
1876/77	1	1	-	36	36	36.00	-/-							-/1
1877	10	15	2	25	145	11.15	-/-							18/16
1878	21	35	2	35	357	10.81	-/-							25/31
1879	13	20	3	37*	125	7.35	-/-							17/6
1880	14	24	1	53	316	13.73	-/1							16/7
1881	7	14	2	36	129	10.75	-/-							9/3
1882	19	33	5	50*	294	10.50	-/1							22/22
1883	12	20	5	28	161	10.73	-/-							12/15
TOTALS	**370**	**645**	**56**	**125**	**9345**	**15.86**	**1/32**	**156.3**	**23**	**390**	**6**	**65.00**	**2-39**	**496/358**

APPENDIX C

PEN-PORTRAITS AND OBITUARIES

1. ARTHUR HAYGARTH 1877

It was the practice of Arthur Haygarth, the compiler of *Scores and Biographies* to present a short biography of any cricketer who played at Lord's. Edward Pooley's first appearance there was for Middlesex against MCC in 1864. This piece was written some thirteen years later.

EDWARD POOLEY's first match at Lord's. Was born at Richmond in Surrey, February 13th 1843. Height 5ft 6in, and weight 9st; afterwards 10st 6lbs or 11 st. Is a fine free and showy batsman, with plenty of confidence and has made many brilliant scores in a rapid manner.

In the field he was at first often at long leg or cover point, but he soon took to keeping wicket and succeeded the far-famed Tom Lockyer in that important post with the Surrey Eleven. In that position he is one of the best that has ever appeared, though it must be observed (in justice to other wicket-keepers), that many of the matches in which he has distinguished himself have taken place on the comparatively slow ground of Kennington Oval, and that most of his marvellous feats have come off against J Southerton's slow and "tempting insinuators".

In the Sussex v Surrey match, July 6th 1868, at The Oval: he stumped 4 and caught 8!! And in the following match, played July 9th 1868, at Gravesend, between Surrey and Kent, he stumped 4 and caught 4!! Astonishing performances in the following matches. In the Surrey v Middlesex match, August 19th 1875, he stumped 2 and caught 6 and in the MCC v Surrey match, July 16th 1876, he stumped 4 and caught 4 &c., &c His bowling is slow lobs, but with these he does not excel. Pooley resided some time at Peckham, and first played with the East Surrey Club, which held its meetings at the Rosemary Branch Inn. He appeared for his native county when very young but did not play regularly in that famous Eleven until about 1865, first assisting Middlesex. In 1862 he was engaged as a bowler to the Surrey Club, but only remained one season. In 1864, or about that time, he opened a cricket and cigar store at 2 Barford Terrace, Liverpool Road, at Islington, in which year also he was engaged as a bowler by the newly formed Middlesex club (meeting then at Islington) and thus appeared at "Headquarters" in the present match for that county. In 1864, also, he was (it is believed) Secretary to another New All England Eleven which started that year, but particulars could not be obtained   In April and May 1865 and 6, he was with Lord Massereene at Belfast, Ireland, but a list of his other engagements (if he took any) could not be procured. In 1867, he scored (it is stated) 1148, nearly, but not quite all in good matches. At the wicket, the same season, he, it was said, stumped and caught for Surrey, the United South of England, and other matches, no fewer than 120 wickets!! On September 2nd 1867, a grand match was played for his benefit on Richmond Green, namely, the United South of England Eleven v 22 of Richmond. Resides at Kennington. His brother F Pooley appeared as a Surrey Colt in 1875 and for the county in 1876 [Another account put E Pooley as having been born in 1842, but which date is correct cannot be said for certain, no positive information having been sent on application.]

2. W G GRACE 1891

In his *Cricket,* published by Arrowsmith in 1891, W G Grace has a section on *Cricketers I have met* in which he comments on the better-known of his contemporaries. These are his comments on Pooley.

EDWARD POOLEY was born at Richmond, Surrey, 13th February 1843. His height was 5ft 6in ; weight around 10 1/2st He was a brilliant wicket-keeper and did splendid work for Surrey. He was worth his position in the eleven for his batting and fielding, but after Lockyer retired he became indispensable[sic] to them for his wicket-keeping alone. As a batsman he was a fine free hitter, and many a time he made a good score when it was badly wanted. He could bowl lobs at a pinch, but they could not be considered first-rate, and I know on several occasions they were very severely handled. When Southerton was bowling and he wicket-keeping they were an effective combination, and he brought off some remarkable catches.

His best stumping records were also made with that bowler, although, rather strangely, one of the, if not the finest was when they were opposed to each other, he playing for Surrey, Southerton for Sussex. In that match he stumped four and caught eight! For the United South he was just as successful, keeping up his wonderful form until his hands gave way. Afterwards he rather shied at fast bowling, although when compelled to, he would face it as well as any man living.

It was intensely amusing to watch him go out and inspect the wicket in later days, and then return and say: "First-rate wicket, sir; slow bowling is sure to come off today." After he had done it two or three times it became rather a standing joke in the eleven, and no matter how slight the inspection of a wicket before a match, someone was sure to remark: "A slow bowler's wicket today , Pooley."

Once or twice he was thought to have been too eager in appealing to the umpire for a decision and was accused of trying to entrap the batsman. My experience of him never showed that: and if he had exceeded the laws I should certainly put it down more to keenness to win than a desire to overreach. He was always on the alert to stump or run out a batsman if he moved his foot before the ball was dead, but the batsman had only himself to blame if it came off, and if a mistake had been made the umpire was more to blame than Pooley.

Pooley was one of the former cricketers interviewed by A W Pullin, who wrote under the pen-name of 'Old Ebor', for his *Talks with Old English Cricketers*, published in 1900. Although it contains several self-evident inaccuracies and possibly several more that are less obvious, it has misled cricket writers and obituarists for a hundred years and consequently a number of misconceptions about Pooley's life have been perpetuated. Known errors of fact are in italic script.

"It was the workhouse, sir or the river. I was at Charing Cross hospital five months with rheumatic fever. The doctors did not think I should come out alive. But old Pooley is tough. I got round, and was discharged, cured. Immediately afterwards I had an attack of influenza which left me very weak. While in that state I met with an accident to my back, which compelled me to go into the Marylebone Infirmary. For about a year I was unable to work. Sponge on my friends I could not, neither could I become a burden to my relatives. I spent a night in the streets deliberating what to do. Then I went into the Lambeth Workhouse."

This was the predicament which the famous old Surrey cricketer, Ted Pooley, had to face in the winter of 1898. He had to choose between a plunge into pauperism or the icy Thames. Like a man he chose the braver part.

The dawn of 1899 saw Pooley with circumstances changed for the better, thanks to the exertions of friends and the press. But before another winter arrived an old enemy of his, rheumatism, had again seized him in its relentless clutch. Once more he sought refuge in the pauper's home. This time some of the daily papers discovered that he had died of cancer of the liver at Brighton. Pooley had the satisfaction of reading his own obituary notice, a piece of luck given to few men. He was at the time as comfortable as rheums and workhouse regulations permit.

It is not the writer's inclination to inquire whether or no Edward Pooley's misfortunes have been wholly unavoidable. Popular cricketers sometimes go to the wall, in which event they are occasionally what a thoughtless public makes them. The past generation of great professionals ought not on fairness to be judged by the present. Education, social surroundings, moral guidance, and influence are higher now than they were in the days when Pooley was young and frisky. Edward Pooley is now a famous old cricketer down on his luck. Those who derived pleasure from his play in days that were earlier will surely sympathise with him in the misfortunes of his later years.

One characteristic of Pooley in his younger days has in no way diminished. He has the same jaunty mien and airy cheerfulness as of old. There is nothing naturally despondent about Ted Pooley's temperament. It could only have been under a temporary fit of extreme depression that he came to contemplate the dread alternative, "The workhouse or the river?"

Edward Pooley was born at Richmond, Surrey, on February 13, 1838. The standard chronicles of the game give the year as 1843, but *Pooley says that is an error for which his father was responsible. 'I don't blame the old man, who is dead and gone. But the fact is that when I was asked for date and year of birth he said I should look more of a colt if I took five years off - which I did.'*

Fifty years ago Pooley played cricket on Richmond Green as the champion of local schoolboys, for stakes of half-a-crown and so on - stakes which, he says, sometimes took a week or ten days to collect. In after years he often played on the same green for £5 a match, his wage as a professional cricketer.

"Yet," says he, "I never dreamed at one time of going out to play as a professional cricketer, I was apprenticed in a soap-merchant's office. The term was for five years, but at the end of three I had had enough of it, so I threw it up, played in a Colts' match at the Oval and then accepted an engagement as a professional cricketer at Perth. In 1861, I had my first trial with the Surrey county team. About the time the first English team to visit Australia was being talked about, H. H. Stephenson, the captain of the team asked me to be one of the side. I did not like to go. To tell the truth, I was doing a bit of sweethearting at that time.

"After playing with Surrey a short time, I assisted Middlesex, but Mr Burrup, the Surrey secretary, got me back again and installed me in the Surrey team. I do not recollect why I left Surrey, but I do remember I was with Middlesex for two years, and that Mr Burrup fetched me back."

To those who chiefly knew Pooley as a wicket-keeper of over twenty years standing, it will be a surprise to be told that he was originally played as a bowler, though he knew little about bowling, and that his natural bent was discovered by accident. Says he:-
"I was chosen as a right-arm bowler, but Lor' bless yer, guv'nor, I had never bowled a ball in a match except slows. I almost laugh now to think of it. Of course, I could get a few runs, and fielded very well at long-leg. *My introduction to wicket-keeping would be about the year 1863.* Old Tom Lockyer's hands were bad and he could not take his usual place behind the sticks. *Mr F P Miller, the Surrey captain was in a quandary as to who should relieve him, so I, saucy-like as usual, went up to him and said, 'Mr Miller, let me have a try.' 'You? What do you know about wicket-keeping? Have you ever kept wicket at all? was Mr Miller's remark. 'No, never, but I should like to try,' I replied. 'Nonsense,' said he,* when just at that moment H H Stephenson came up and remarked, 'Let the

young 'un have a go, sir.' Mr Miller thereupon relented. I donned the gloves, quickly got two or three wickets, and seemed so much at home that Tom Lockyer was delighted, and said I was born to keep wicket and would have to be his successor in the Surrey team. What he said came true.'

Pooley's hands are the most remarkable the writer has seen, The oldest living cricketer, and in his day the best of wicket-keepers, Mr Herbert Jenner-Fust "kept" without gloves, yet his hands today are shapely and undamaged, with one slight exception. George Pinder has some of his joints distorted, evidences of the hard knocks that he encountered. But Pooley - another of the great triumvirate of Pinder, Pooley, and Pilling - possesses two fists that are mere lumps of deformity.

Every finger on the two hands has been broken; so have the two thumbs. The joints are knotted and gnarled in a way that suggests the thumbscrew rather than the stumper's gloves. The writer suggests that some of the deformity might be due to rheumatism. "Not a bit of it," replies Pooley, bringing a maimed fist down with a heavy thump on the table. "There's no rheumatics there; it's all cricket," All the same, rheumatism has had something to do with the strange deformity

Chatting carelessly on, Pooley says: "In my younger days I was once introduced to Jem Mace. I was keeping wicket at a match at Lord's - on a pitch which at the time was so bad that you could put your finger between the cracks on the surface. A ball shot up and knocked out three of my teeth. At lunch-time I was going to wash my damaged mouth when I was told a gentleman wanted to be introduced to me. He proved to be Jem Mace. 'Pooley,' said he, 'I would rather stand up against any man in England for an hour than take your place behind the wicket for five minutes. I heard that ball strike you as if it had hit a brick wall.'

"But these accidents are nothing. They are all in the game and stumpers then thought little of them as they do now. The worst accident I had was at Jersey, when my nose was broken. Ted Willsher was bowling to a batsman who had as much idea of batting as a crossing-sweeper. Willsher brought Charlwood to short-leg for a catch, and sent the batsman one rather wide on the leg-side. The striker turned round, made a mighty swipe at the ball, missed it, and caught me full on the nose. I dropped like a log, insensible. When I came to myself a doctor was grating the bones in my broken nasal organ with a view to repairing the damage. Ugh!

"Another extraordinary incident, more serious in its results, occurred in Surrey v Sussex at Brighton in 1871. Jupp threw the ball in to me to run a man out. The ball caught me on the top of the forefinger. For the moment I took no notice of the blow. We used to play at that time in flannel jackets, and on putting my hand up for a catch shortly afterwards I found that blood was running through the arm of my jacket. Taking off my glove, I then saw that *the bone of the finger was broken, and protruded through the skin.* A surgeon was called, and *the joint put into splints, and he gave me the discomforting assurance that I should not be able to play cricket for months.*

"The Canterbury Festival, which I had not missed for years, came on just afterwards. I wired to Mr I D Walker that I could not possibly play, but he replied that I was to attend and I would be paid whether I played or not. Accordingly I went, and on reaching the ground found that four or five players had travelled by the Dover express and had been carried past Canterbury. I was enjoying a comfortable pint when Mr Walker came up a quarter of an hour before luncheon and asked me to go in at once. I did so, with boots unlaced and no pads on; and before I was out my score was 93, in recognition of which a collection was made for me on the ground. When my innings was over I found that my injury had caused a lump in my armpit as big as a walnut. I was mightily alarmed for the time being, but, fortunately, my cricket was not seriously interfered with.

"Mention of Canterbury reminds me that Mr C I Thornton, whom I have always regarded as the hardest hitter the world has seen, and myself once went to see how many runs we could get in a certain time. *At the end of half an hour the score was 130 or 140.* Mr Thornton hit one ball over a tree into the hop-gardens....I tried to throw a ball over that tree afterwards and could not manage it.

"I think I may say that Mr Thornton did not like me behind the wicket when he was batting. He used to say, 'If you were not there, Pooley, I could step out a bit, but if I do and miss I shall be stumped.' In one match against Kent we got Mr Thornton's wicket in a way that caused us much glee. He came in, without pads as usual, and remarked to me, 'Ted, I'll hit Street right out of the ground first ball.' 'All right; do, sir,' I replied. I gave Jim the tip that Mr Thornton intended to step out to the first delivery, and told him to drop it very short. Street did so, and Mr Thornton, stepping out, missed it by yards - more or less. He made no attempt to regain his crease, but looking round at me, said ruefully, 'All right, Ted; you've had me this time.'"

Certain unpleasantness occurred in one of the Yorkshire v Surrey matches at Sheffield twenty years or so ago, concerning which there were allegations of gambling. The facts, as now given by Pooley, show that the suspicions that existed were unjust.

"I was accused," says he, "of having tried to lose Surrey the match. What happened was this. I went down to Sheffield on the Sunday night, ready for the match the following day, and stayed at our usual hostelry, kept by Jim Darley. Jim said, 'Well, lad, what sort of a side have you brought?' I replied, 'Jim, my boy, we haven't got a chance with you, but I'll tell you what I will do - I'll bet a bottle of champagne that I get more runs than any one on your side you like to name.' Jupp chimes in 'Only one bottle, Ted? Make it two, then we can have one each for breakfast.' I agreed; we two would have a bottle each against the score of any two Yorkshiremen. The consequence was that 'old Mary' Lockwood, one of the very best men Yorkshire ever turned out, and Andrew Greenwood were named as the Yorkshire pair. As luck would have it, *I got the most runs*, and Jupp and I won the two bottles - which we duly had for breakfast the next day.

"Well, this innocent bet was magnified by gossip into a bet of £50 made by me against Surrey winning the match. There was a row about it, and I was indignant and made remarks, as any one else would have done under the circumstances. *I was never a gambler on cricket.* As to our couple of bottles, it was all in good friendship, for Lockwood and Andrew Greenwood were at that time two of the best batsmen in England."

There was a match between the Gentlemen and Players at the Oval in June 1869, which the Gentlemen won by 17 runs. Pooley and Wootton made a great effort to pull the game off for the Players. Just before the finish Willsher entered the field with a drink for Pooley, and it was then said that it was done for the purpose of wasting time. What says Pooley?

"It was a race against time. *There were 87 runs to be got* when the ninth wicket fell. I was in good form, while Wootton, who did not usually stay for more than two overs, kept his end up wonderfully well. I hit up 52 in less than an hour , and then Mr C Absolom bowled me off my legs. I can see that ball now as plainly as possible; it was one I ought to have hit. The Gentlemen won by 17 runs about thirteen minutes before the time for drawing stumps. It is perfectly true that Willsher brought me out something to drink, but I do not recollect that anything was said by him to me as to how we should play. Mr Gale has said that the glass of water (was it water?) was an excuse for giving me riding orders - namely to play for a win and not to draw. But I don't remember him saying anything of the kind. Willsher brought me a drink in the usual way and I needed no riding orders. Having got so near, it was only likely we should play to win and not to draw the match. There was certainly no idea of wasting time. Willsher was not the man to save a match by that means.

"Perhaps the most amusing incident that I can remember in my cricketing experiences occurred at Whitehaven, in a match Grace's XI *v* a local Twenty, who had the assistance of Barlow and the late Jack Platts - he of the fatal Summers match. Platts was batting when the ball stuck in his hands. W R Gilbert sang out, 'Get to it, Ted' and as I was about to do so Platts deliberately put the ball in his trousers, without saying a word. He knew, however, he had done wrong, for when I said, 'Jack, what's up?' he immediately ran away from his wicket. He was followed by nearly all the members of the Eleven, and a most comic race it was - a set of fielders running after a batsman all round the enclosure. In running the ball slipped down Platt's trousers, and he tried to kick it out, but before he could do so one of the fielders got hold of him, and he was held down while the ball was taken out of his trousers, before it could touch the ground.

"It was a most laughable and extraordinary incident, but the sequel was even more so. Platts walked coolly back to his wicket and prepared to continue his innings. 'What's your game now, Jack?' I asked; 'you know you're out.' 'Ask the umpires,' said he. I did so, and the artists gave him 'not out' on the ground that they could not see what happened! Yet, as a fact, he was out in three ways - handling the ball, obstructing the field, and caught."

The writer here may interpolate a remark on this incident. Platt always declared that he never handled the ball. He used to play in an ordinary grey shirt, and his trousers always came above his belt an inch or two, so there was plenty of room for a ball to lodge. He played the ball into his shirt. When he started to run it was with the intention of jerking the ball out, but "it went the wrong way, down his trousers!"

"In the same match at Whitehaven," continues Pooley, " I ran Barlow out when he was two yards out of his ground. In trying to get home the end of his bat stuck, and Barlow received such a blow that he fell over insensible. We gave him a drink of brandy - though he was a teetotaller - and on coming round the first thing he said was, 'I am not out, am I?' On being told that he was out, didn't he look cross! He took the loss of his wicket more keenly than the temporary loss of his senses."

Pooley was a member of the fourth English team that went to Australia in 1876 under the captaincy of James Lillywhite. The team also visited New Zealand, and while there Pooley was under a cloud, and had to endure compulsory separation from his colleagues for some time. He is not afraid of referring to the matter now. It appears that there was a bet on a certain match which the touring party won. The gentleman who made it refused to pay, and a disturbance and an assault ensued. By all accounts, the gentleman who refused to pay was the worst, and though there was undoubtedly an assault, Pooley says that *two members of the team, both now dead, did the most damage.* Be that as it may, Pooley was detained and put on trial. He was acquitted and he says now that the decision gave so much local satisfaction that a purse of 50 guineas was subscribed for him, a watch and chain were presented to him and he was driven round the town in a four-in-hand like a conquering hero.

Like other old cricketers, Pooley got little 'fat' out of some of the cricket excursions at home. Just one instance in proof of the fact that the jolly life of a pro in the old days was not always attended with financial success:-

"I remember we once played at Edinburgh with the old United. When Mortlock and I got back to the Elephant and Castle we had 1s 4d in our pockets between us. We said if that was the result of going to play cricket in Scotland, we preferred to play at Kennington Oval"

In addition to the chief teams, the United and All England, there was a team run by Fred Caesar for a brief time, of which Pooley acted as secretary. That team once played Tom Sherman's team at the Oval for the championship and won it. The chief thing Pooley remembers about these enterprises is that "the money was divided - and there was a rare bother over the division."

Humphrey, Jupp, and Pooley used to play single wicket matches against elevens in various parts of the South, and Pooley says the trio were never beaten, though he admits they found it very hard work. Pooley is the only survivor of the triumvirate.

In addition to the journey to Australia already mentioned, Pooley was one of Willsher's team that went to America in 1868. George Freeman and he had bunks in the same cabin. The pair were very ill on the journey, but even Pooley had to laugh when George, in the throes of sea-sickness, moaned out, "Ted, what an ass I must be. As if I could not get plenty of cricket in Yorkshire without coming out on a sea like this!"

The men who made this journey were Willsher, Shaw, Pooley, Jupp, Humphrey, Charlwood, Jim Lillywhite, Tarrant, Jack Smith of Cambridge, George Freeman and Joe Rowbotham. Of these only Shaw, Pooley, and Lillywhite, are now alive. Rowbotham was the last to join the majority, his death occurring in December last. Pooley speaks of Rowbotham with good-humoured familiarity as "Old Tarpot." Asked why such an eminently respected cricketer should be so christened, he said that no matter how ill other people were on board, Joe Rowbotham never missed a meal. He stuck to everything he ate so well that they nicknamed him "Old Tarpot."

The Rev. Canon M'Cormick made 137 in North v South at Canterbury on August 3, 1868, when Pooley was keeping wicket. When near the end of the innings, Pooley said to him, "Well, sir, this is the most extraordinary experience I ever had at cricket. All the time you have been in I have scarcely taken a single ball at the wicket. If the ball was straight you played it, and if it was crooked you hit it." "That," adds Pooley now ,"was quite true."

Pooley pays to George Pinder the compliment of saying he was the smartest man at taking a ball at the wicket he ever saw, though he adds that the famous Yorkshireman did not watch for the "psychological moment" when the batsman had his toe off the crease. His contemporaries say that Pooley himself was better at slow bowling than fast, but it is perhaps only human on Pooley's part to say that he doesn' t hold the same opinion, and to remind those who do that he kept wicket to Freeman and Tarrant, "two of the fastest bowlers in England." His testimony to George Freeman coincides with that of many others who knew him, for he says, "I reckoned Freeman to be the best fast bowler I saw in all my life." Pooley likes the older days, which is perhaps natural, and says:-

"Some time ago a few of us old cronies were at Lord's together, and we exchanged opinions as to the merits of past and present-day cricket. We were all of the opinion that it is not as good as it used to be. Why, a man ought to be able to keep wicket blindfolded now. The wickets are so good, and you get nearly every ball on the off-side barely stump high. Some of the wickets of my time were like turnpike roads, and you had to look after your eyes I can tell you."

It may be said from this that Pooley is a praiser of times past. So be it. When the present generation of cricketers become greybeards will they not think that the best days were those when they were young?

4. OBITUARY FROM 'THE TIMES' 19 July 1907

The once famous Surrey wicket-keeper, Edward Pooley, died yesterday in Lambeth Infirmary. He had for some years past been in great poverty, and latterly in bad health. No one who follows the game at all closely will need to be told that in his day he was one of the most popular of the Surrey players. Succeeding Tom Lockyer in the Surrey XI in the 60s, he had a long and brilliant career, finally dropping out of the team after the season of 1883. Beyond question he was one of the finest wicket-keepers who ever appeared. When in his prime he had no equal against slow and medium pace bowling; but to very fast bowling he was not considered as good as George Pinder and Tom Plumb. It is only fair to say, however, that his opportunities of keeping wicket to bowlers of great pace were rather restricted. In a match between Surrey and Sussex at The Oval in 1868 he got rid of 12 batsmen - six in each innings - this being still the record in first-class cricket. Of the 12 he caught 8 and stumped 4. As a batsman he was quite first rate and he would have made many more runs if he had not so often suffered from damaged hands. His highest score in a big match was 125 for the Players of the South against the Gentlemen of the South at the Oval in 1871. He was born on February 13 1838 and was thus in his 70th year. While he was playing cricket he was thought to be five years younger than his real age. The mistake arose from the fact that when he began his career his father thought he would have a better chance if he represented himself as younger than he really was.

5. OBITUARY FROM 'CRICKET' 25 July 1907

The statistics quoted for Surrey have changed since 1907, principally because of reclassification of matches formerly deemed first-class

OBITUARY.

E. POOLEY.

Edward Pooley, who was born at Richmond, in Surrey, on February 13th, 1838, died in Lambeth Infirmary on Thursday morning last. *Scores and Biographies* (viii. 430) says of him:—'' Is a fine free and showy batsman, with plenty of confidence, and has made many brilliant scores in a rapid manner. In the field he was at first often long-leg or cover-point, but he soon took to keeping wicket, and succeeded the far-famed Tom Lockyer in that important post with the Surrey Eleven. In that position he is one of the best that has ever appeared, though, it must be observed (in justice to other wicket-keepers), that many of the matches in which he has distinguished himself have taken place on the comparatively slow ground of Kennington Oval, and that most of his marvellous feats have come off against J. Southerton's slow and 'tempting insinuators.' "

Pooley played his first match for Surrey in 1861, and must have been a very good cricketer even then for he was invited to accompany H. H. Stephenson's team to Australia in the autumn. He did not then make the journey, however, postponing his visit until he went out as a member of Lillywhite's side thirteen years later. His connection with Surrey lasted from 1861 until 1883, during which time he appeared in 261 matches for the County, playing 422 completed innings for 6,728 runs, and averaging 15·93. In 1864 and 1865 he assisted Middlesex also, and it was as a member of that team that he played his first match at Lord's—against M.C.C. and Ground, in July, 1864. His name will be found in twelve Middlesex matches, including the first played by the County since its re-formation—against Buckinghamshire, at Newport Pagnell. Between 1866 and 1879 he took part in twenty-five matches between the Gentlemen and the Players, his highest score being 86 at the Oval in 1867, and his average for the whole series the good one of 19·09. His largest innings for Surrey was 97 against Cambridge University, at Fenner's, in 1874,

but in great matches he twice exceeded that total, making 125 for Players of South v. Gentlemen of South, at Kennington three years earlier, and 111 in a match between the same sides (the Gentlemen being allowed fourteen men) at Southampton in 1865 : on the latter occasion Japp scored 216, the Players making 483 and winning by an innings and 179 runs. One of Pooley's greatest batting feats was performed in the Canterbury Week of 1871, when, in a match between North and South, he scored 93 whilst suffering from a fractured finger against the bowling of Alfred and

J. C. Shaw, Martin McIntyre, Farrands, and Mr. W. M. Rose.

Pooley's fame, however, rests upon his skill as a wicket-keeper. In having to follow so great a master of the art as Lockyer he was tried very highly, and that he suffered by comparison with his great predecessor is eloquent testimony to his ability. With Pinder and Plumb he ranked for many years as the best wicket-keeper in England : he was better than either of his rivals against slow bowling, though less used than them to fast. In four consecutive matches for Surrey, in 1868, he caught 16 and

stumped 16, taking 20 wickets in two successive matches—eight caught and four stumped v. Sussex, at the Oval, and four caught and four stumped v. Kent, at Gravesend. Against the last-mentioned side at Kennington ten years later, he caught two and stumped eight, against Middlesex on the same ground in 1875 he caught six and stumped two, and against M.C.C. and Ground, at Lord's in 1878, he caught four and stumped four. His performance in the match with Sussex in 1863, when he took as many as twelve wickets—six in each innings—has stood as a record for first-class cricket for four decades. As showing how prolific " a snapper-up of unconsidered trifles " he was, it may be added that in great matches he has taken more wickets than any other wicket-keeper, David Hunter alone excepted. During his career his hands were very severely knocked about, and at one time or another he had every finger either broken or dislocated. He frequently played when it would have been wiser for him to have stood down owing to his injuries, but he was so fond of the game that he always played whenever it was humanly possible to do so. He was accorded two benefit matches—U.S.E.E. v. XXII. of Richmond, at Richmond, in 1867, and North v. South, at the Oval, in 1883, the latter bringing him in about £500.

Pooley was undoubtedly one of the very best cricketers in England three or four decades ago, and it is sad to think that his last few years should have been spent in a workhouse. He did not order his life well, unfortunately, and had only himself to blame for his misfortune. But he could be a very entertaining and genial man when he wished, so that at times his good humour almost appeared to atone for his failings.

MATCHES TO COME AT THE OVAL.

July 11—Benefit of Early Closing Association | Aug. 4—Surrey Club v. Epsom.
12—Surrey v. Nottingham. | 19—Surrey v. Kent.
18—Surrey v. Lancashire. | 17—Surrey and Middlesex v. England—
22—Gentlemen of the South v. Players. | for the Benefit of Julius Cæsar.
29—Private Banks v. Joint Stock. | 24—Surrey v. Yorkshire.
20—Surrey v. Middlesex. | 27—Surrey Club v. Banstead.

SURREY COUNTY CRICKET CLUB,
KENNINGTON OVAL.

SURREY v. SUSSEX.
On MONDAY and TUESDAY, JULY 6th and 7th, 1868.

SUSSEX.	First Innings.		Second Innings.	
C. H. Smith, Esq...	c Pooley, b Bristow ..	5	not out..............	47
Payne	c Pooley, b Bristow ..	17	c Pooley, b Bristow ..	17
Hon. F. Pelham ..	l b w, b Sewell.......	5	b Bristow...........	2
James Lillywhite..	c Pooley, b Bristow	32	st Pooley, b Bristow	0
— Greenhill, Esq...	st Pooley, b Bristow	15	b Sewell.............	0
Charlwood	c Pooley, b Bristow ..	7	c Pooley, b Sewell	0
Killick..............	c Pooley, b Bristow ..	8	c Pooley, b Sewell	2
Wells	c Street, b Sewell	1	st Pooley, b Sewell ...	5
Ellis................	c Jupp, b Bristow	4	b Sewell..............	0
Southerton	b Sewell	0	st Pooley, b Street.....	9
Stubberfield	not out	4	c Nightingale, b Street	9
	b 1, l-b 1, w , n-b,	2	b 8, l-b 4, w , n-b,	12
	Total....	**98**	**Total....**	**128**

SURREY.	First Innings.		Second Innings.	
Humphrey	c & b Southerton ...	8	c Smith, b Stubberfield	13
Jupp	c Southerton, b Lillywhite	14	not out...............	37
Pooley	c Ellis, b Lillywhite	15	c Greenhill, b Lillywhite	10
Stephenson	c Charlwood, b Southerton	37	run out	18
Mortlock...........	c Greenhill, b Lillywhite	15	not out...............	24
Bristow	c Payne, b Stubberfield	0		
J. Noble, Esq......	b Southerton	8		
C. Calvert Esq....	c Wells, b Lillywhite	13		
Sewell	l b w, b Southerton...	0		
J. Nightingale.....	not out	2		
J. Street	c Ellis, b Lillywhite	14		
	b , lb , w , n-b,		b , lb , w , n-b,	
	Total	**126**	**Total..**	**102**

Umpires: Willsher & Luck.

This Obituary was duplicated in the Richmond and Twickenham Times *on 3 August 1907*

EDWARD POOLEY.

This once-famous Surrey wicket-keeper and one-time licensee died yesterday week at Lambeth Infirmary at the age of sixty-nine years. Very few people of to-day are aware that about thirty-five years ago "Ted" Pooley kept a beerhouse in the Kew Foot Road, Richmond, Surrey, called the "Albany," which has long ceased to exist as a public-house, and the premises—adjoining the athletic ground—are now in the occupation of Mr. Wimple, an upholsterer, though the old skittle-alley is now used by Mr. Clark, furniture dealer, who very kindly allowed the writer to inspect the premises. Those were the rosy days of the Surrey crack wicket-keeper, and many of the old Surrey Eleven could be seen at the "Albany" in those days; indeed, one of George Clifford's single-wicket matches was made in the old house, and Ted Pooley was a noted figure about Richmond, where he was born, in those days. Jack Swan, who kept the "Princess Head," at one time was a noted friend of Ted Pooley, and he and George Clifford, now of the "Cricketers," Richmond Green, played along with Pooley, Humphrey, and Jupp in the match Yorkshire v. Surrey at the Oval in 1874, when Jupp, who was in those days quite as much the backbone of Surrey batting as Tom Hayward is to-day, carried his bat throughout both innings for 40 odd and 109 not out, a feat that has never even yet been equalled in a first-class match. In those days Humphrey, Jupp, and Pooley often played eleven others at single wicket, and all three of them were famous members of the old United South of England Eleven along with Southerton, Lillywhite, and Frank Silcock. Ted Pooley played for Middlesex at one time, and afterwards succeeded Tom Lockyer as Surrey's wicket-keeper. He, Jupp, and Humphrey had to bear the brunt of the Surrey batting in the seventies, and Southerton and Street the bowling. Whether Pooley, Pinder, Plumb, Phillips, or Pilling was the best wicket-keeper of his day is a matter of opinion, but there is no doubt about Pooley's cleverness behind the stumps and his capacity for getting runs in front of them. W. G. Grace played on and off with or against Pooley from 1866 to 1883, when the latter retired and received his benefit. Pooley was made a god of by the Surrey crowd at one time, and, with all his faults, he was a very interesting figure to the end of his days. More than once he had been reported as dead, and it was said that when he was at death's door in a certain hospital he called for a pint of beer, which restored him to health but not to wealth. It is sad that Pooley, as well as Jupp and the two Humphreys, should have died in poverty, but such was the case, though at one time they were the pets of the multitude. Pooley was nearly the last of the old school of cricketers, and no useful purpose would be served in comparing them with the giants of to-day. In Pooley's opinion and that of his contemporaries there never will be another cricketer like W. G. Grace, who was once playing in Hertfordshire under an assumed name, and had scored over a century, when Ted Pooley unexpectedly appeared on the scene and disclosed "W. G.'s" real identity. Pooley was once or twice suspended from the Surrey County team for one cause or another; nevertheless, he was at one time indispensable, and could get runs as well and as fast as most players. Even with damaged hands at Canterbury he scored something like 90 runs in a North v. South match, and was not out 46, with "W. G." 50 odd, in the 1876 North v. South match, played for the benefit of his old comrade Tom Humphrey.

Pooley always stood close up to the wicket, whether the bowling was fast or slow, and he steadfastly refused to stand back, as is the custom to-day, to fast bowling. The name of Pooley will not be soon forgotten by those who knew him.

7. OBITUARY FROM 'WISDEN' 1908

EDWARD POOLEY, the once-famous Surrey wicket-keeper, died in Lambeth Infirmary on July 18, 1907. He had for a long time been in very poor circumstances and was often compelled to seek the shelter of the workhouse. Born on February 13, 1838, he was in his 70th year. All through his cricket career it was generally supposed that he was born in 1843 and the real date of his birth was only made known by himself in his interview in *Old English Cricketers*. It seems that when he determined to take up cricket professionally his father thought that he would have a better chance if he knocked a few years off his age. Thus, though regarded at the time as quite a young player, he was over 23 when in May 1861, he played at The Oval for a team of Surrey Colts against the Gentlemen of the Surrey Club with Hayes and Heartfield. At that time his future fame as a wicket-keeper was unthought of, and presumably he was tried for his batting. Playing on the same side were Harry Jupp and the still surviving J Bristow. In 1862 Pooley was engaged as one of the bowlers at the Oval, but his regular connection with the Surrey XI did not begin until about 1865. In the meantime he played for Middlesex, making his first appearance at Lord's for that county against the MCC on July 25, 1864. The match was a memorable one inasmuch as Grundy and Wootton got Middlesex out in the first innings for a total of 20. The story of how he came to succeed Tom Lockyer is graphically told by himself in *Old English Cricketers*......

In 1866, Pooley established his position as one of the leading professionals of the day and thenceforward he remained a member of the Surrey XI for 17 years, finally dropping out in 1883. His great days as a wicket-keeper date from the time of the late James Southerton's connection with Surrey in 1867. The two men helped each other enormously. Southerton's slow bowling with a pronounced off-break was then something comparatively new and while batsmen were learning to play him the wicket-keeper naturally had great chances. It is safe to say that no wicket-keeper then before the public could have assisted Southerton to the extent that Pooley did. He was quick as lightning and with all his brilliancy very safe. Partly from lack of opportunity he was not quite so good as Pinder or Tom Plumb to very fast bowling, but to slow bowling he was in his day supreme. Two or three pages of *Wisden* could easily be filled with details of his doings, but it is sufficient to say that the record of the greatest number of wickets obtained in a first-class match still stands to his credit after an interval of nearly 40 years. In the Surrey v Sussex match at the Oval in July 1868, he got rid of 12 batsmen, stumping one and catching five in the first innings and stumping three and catching three in the second. Curiously enough, Southerton was in the Sussex team in this match, players in those days being allowed to play for two counties in the same season if qualified by birth for one and residence for the other. The rule was changed just afterwards and Southerton threw in his lot with Surrey. Apart from his wicket-keeping Pooley was a first-rate bat, free in style with fine driving power and any amount of confidence. He made many good scores and would without doubt have been a much greater run-getter if he had not been so constantly troubled by damaged hands. During the Canterbury week of 1871, he played an innings of 93 when suffering with a broken finger. Of the faults of private character that marred Pooley's career and were the cause of the poverty in which he spent the later years of his life there is no need now to speak. He was in many ways his own enemy, but even to the last he had a geniality and sense of humour that to a certain extent condoned his weaknesses.

APPENDIX D

THE POOLEY FAMILY TREE

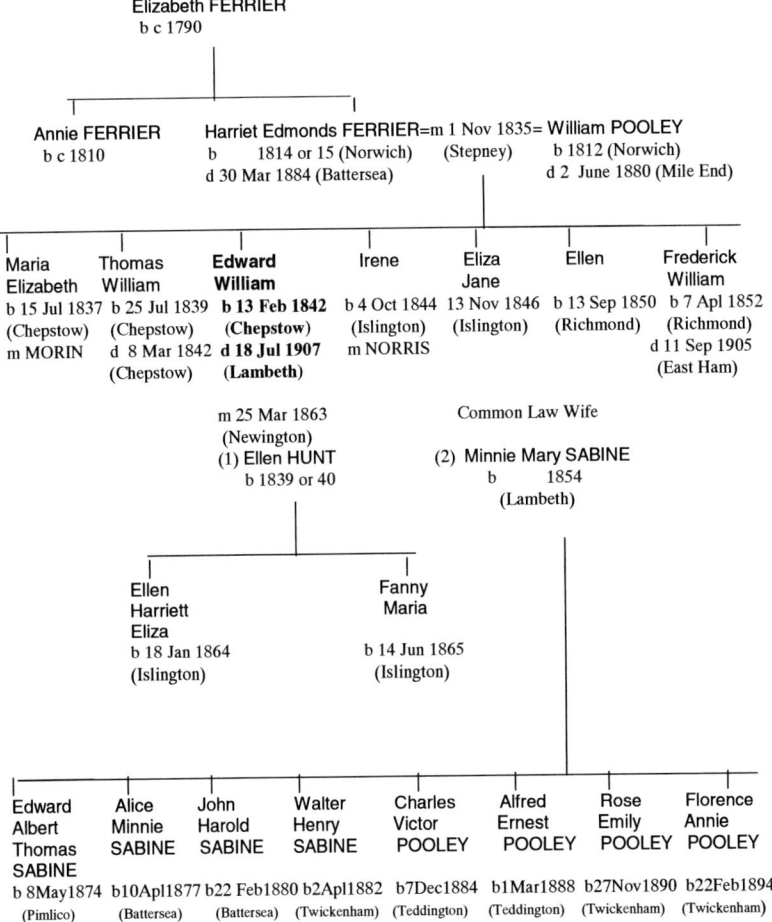

Elizabeth FERRIER
b c 1790

Annie FERRIER
b c 1810

Harriet Edmonds FERRIER=m 1 Nov 1835= William POOLEY
b   1814 or 15 (Norwich)   (Stepney)   b 1812 (Norwich)
d 30 Mar 1884 (Battersea)   d 2 June 1880 (Mile End)

Maria   Thomas   Edward   Irene   Eliza   Ellen   Frederick
Elizabeth   William   William   Jane   William
b 15 Jul 1837 b 25 Jul 1839 b 13 Feb 1842   b 4 Oct 1844   13 Nov 1846   b 13 Sep 1850 b 7 Apl 1852
(Chepstow)   (Chepstow)   (Chepstow)   (Islington)   (Islington)   (Richmond)   (Richmond)
m MORIN   d 8 Mar 1842 d 18 Jul 1907   m NORRIS   d 11 Sep 1905
               (Chepstow)   (Lambeth)   (East Ham)

m 25 Mar 1863   Common Law Wife
(Newington)
(1) Ellen HUNT   (2) Minnie Mary SABINE
   b 1839 or 40   b   1854
                                              (Lambeth)

Ellen   Fanny
Harriett   Maria
Eliza
b 18 Jan 1864   b 14 Jun 1865
(Islington)   (Islington)

Edward   Alice   John   Walter   Charles   Alfred   Rose   Florence
Albert   Minnie   Harold   Henry   Victor   Ernest   Emily   Annie
Thomas   SABINE   SABINE   SABINE   POOLEY   POOLEY   POOLEY   POOLEY
SABINE
b 8May1874 b10Apl1877 b22 Feb1880 b2Apl1882   b7Dec1884   b1Mar1888 b27Nov1890 b22Feb1894
(Pimlico)   (Battersea) (Battersea) (Twickenham) (Teddington) (Teddington) (Twickenham) (Twickenham)

APPENDIX E

THE POOLEY RESIDENCES

Chapter 12, quoting Byron's *Childe Harold's Pilgrimage*, was headed 'The Wandering Outlaw'. It was intended to refer to Pooley's moral and physical disintegration and his erratic fin-de-siècle meanderings between the end of his playing career and his death in the Workhouse. It would, however, be not inappropriate to apply the quotation to the whole of Pooley's life, as in between playing professional cricket, running into trouble with authority and fathering a large family, he seems to have spent most of his time moving house. His father's peripatetic schoolmastering took Edward to three addresses before he was nine and no two of Edward's own ten children were born at the same address. Census entries reveal further residences. Younger sisters, Irene and Eliza Jane, share the same place of birth in Islington; twenty years later when Edward returned to Islington as a tobacconist, 2 Barford Terrace which Haygarth mentions as Pooley's address in *Scores and Biographies* is confirmed as the birth of eldest daughter, Ellen Harriett Eliza; in 1884 the Wick Road, South Teddington is probably the same as the *Cricketers' Companion*'s Fairfield Cottage, Hampton Wick and it is also likely that the 19 Barton Terrace of Rose's birth and 19 Denmark Road of the 1891 Census are one and the same. Those four instances apart, however, there is no confirmatory evidence of any address at which Pooley lived. In addition, of course, there would be a large number of temporary residences as a result of his professional appointments and domestic and overseas tours. The following list is an indication of the frequency with which he voluntarily or otherwise changed his address, though it makes no claim to be comprehensive as there may well have been additional residences squeezed into the gaps between births and censuses.

Date	Residence	Source of Information
1842	Lower Church Street, Chepstow	Census
1844/46	4 Shepperton Cottages, Islington	Irene and Eliza's birth certificates
1850/51	22 The Green, Richmond	Sister Ellen's birth certificate;Census
1852	Friars Lane, Richmond	Frederick's birth certificate
1861	Perth	History of Perth Cricket Club
1863	Amelia Street, Newington	Marriage certificate
	Old Ford Road, Bow/ Peckham	*Post Office London Directory*

Date	Residence	*Scores and Biographies* Source of Information
1864	2 Barford Terrace, Islington	Daughter Ellen's birth certificate
1865	Belfast	*Scores and Biographies* Newspapers and scorebooks
	82 St James Road, Holloway	Fanny's birth certificate
	Old Ford Road, Bow	*Post Office London Directory*
1868	U S A and Canada	*Scores and Biographies* Reference books
1873	Albany Beerhouse, Kew Foot Road Richmond	Obituary in *Licensing News*
1874	2 Church Street, Pimlico	Son Edward's birth certificate
1876	Richmond	*Scores and Biographies*
1876/77	Australia and New Zealand	Reference books
1877	Richmond	*Scores and Biographies*
1877	8 Verona Street, Battersea	Alice's birth certificate
1880	32 Speke Road, Battersea	John's birth certificate
1882	37 Landseer Street, Battersea	Walter's birth certificate
1884	Wick Road, South Teddington/ Fairfield Cottage, Hampton Wick	Charles' birth certificate *Cricketers' Companion*
1888	Fulwell Road, Teddington	Alfred's birth certificate
1890	19 Barton Cottages, Twickenham	Rose's birth certificate
1891	19 Denmark Road, Twickenham	Census
1894	14 Garfield Road, Twickenham	Florence's birth certificate
1898	Rowton House, Bond Street Renfrew Road Workhouse, Lambeth	Workhouse records
1899	No home Renfrew Road Workhouse, Lambeth	
1900	Rowton House	
1900/01	Renfrew Road Workhouse	
1901/02	Rowton House	
1902/03	Renfrew Road Workhouse	
1903/04	Risbridge Union Workhouse, Suffolk	
1904	Duchy of Cornwall Public House, Bowling Green Street, Kennington	
1904/06	Renfrew Road Workhouse	
1906/07	Workhouse Infirmary	Death certificate and obituaries

APPENDIX F

THE POOLEY FAMILY TODAY

Edward Pooley was one of seven children. He himself had ten and one of those had ten. Since his time Marie Stopes (born in 1880, the same year as his second son, John Harold and as the first Test Match on English soil) and the consequences of her philosophy have hit the scene and exponential continuation of that kind of growth looks unlikely. Large families in the nineteenth century were the norm rather than the exception, partly because of the absence of birth control and partly as an insurance against infant mortality. If all his children and all his grandchildren had continued to propagate at the same rate as Edward and John Harold, then we would be looking at something like a thousand great grandchildren and Appendix D, The Pooley Family Tree, already somewhat contorted to fit the page, would soon reach unmanageable proportions.

This is not, however, primarily a book about the Pooley family, but about Edward Pooley and I have therefore restricted the family tree in Appendix D, give or take the odd member of a previous generation, where known about, to his parents, siblings and children. It would be ungracious, however not to acknowledge the help I have received from one branch of the family, so I thought it apposite to append a note on those Pooleys I have had the privilege of meeting to demonstrate the continuity of the family.

Of the ten children of Edward's fifth child and second son, John Harold (known as Jack), three now survive of whom I have met one, Ronald Victor, the eighth child and youngest son, at the time of writing, a very active 79 year old living in Bracknell. Born in Twickenham, Ron has clear memories of his father playing cricket on Twickenham Green, so the cricket interest certainly continued into a third generation, from Edward's father, William, through Edward himself to Jack. The educational interest, however, did not. Ron was never able to persuade his father to provide the funds required to send him to Grammar School, as recommended by his head teacher. "Just wouldn't part with his money...he liked a few pints....Many a time I argued with him that I wanted to go to Grammar School...but I wasn't so lucky". So the taste for alcohol seems to have been transferred from father to son Jack. Hereditary influences were perhaps stronger in other parts of the family. Ron also recalls that one of his elder brothers, Wallace, as well as having looks almost identical to those of his grandfather, had similar drinking and gambling habits.

The Crimean War apart, Britain enjoyed a virtually unbroken period of peace from the Napoleonic Wars to the end of the century, so Edward had never been near a battlefield - other than domestic ones and those arenas of pseudo-warfare, the cricket fields of England - but his son, Jack fought in the Boer War and Ron distinguished himself in the Second World War as an air gunner flying Lancaster Bombers with the famous 617 squadron. Although he did not take part in what through later publicity became their best-known raid on the Möhne and Eder dams in 1943, it was for an air-raid on Berlin in August of the same year that he was awarded the DFM. Acquainted with, and a great admirer of, Wing Commander Leonard Cheshire (later Baron Cheshire of Woodhall) Ron was demobbed in 1946 after further service in India. His four brothers had all been on active service. All returned safe and well. Civilian life saw Ron take a series of office jobs, most recently as Production Control Supervisor at Bestobell Seals. He retired in 1986 to enjoy his garden and - like the father of a recent Prime Minister - make the occasional garden ornament in his shed.

He married twice and became a father at the relatively late age of 58, when in January 1979, his only child, Natalie Joanne, was born to his second wife, Mavis. Now aged 21 and equipped with three 'A' levels, Edward's great grand-daughter is a Sales and Marketing Assistant with Overland Data, a San Diego based company specialising in tape production and storage, the UK offices of which are in Wokingham.

Margaret Joan, Ronald's younger sister, was also born in Twickenham. Like her elder brother, she found her early career aspirations thwarted through lack of finance, and instead of becoming a hairdresser or florist as she would have wished, found herself in the somewhat less glamorous area of bakery and spark-plugs. She married in 1943: her sons Michael and Robert were born in 1945 and 1956. Michael pursued a career with the GPO, later British Telecom, and, after a series of managerial posts in central London, took early retirement in 1996. His daughters, Edward's great-great-granddaughters, are on the way to becoming established in their own careers. Emma, born in 1975, is a psychology graduate of Portsmouth University, now with the AA and looking towards a career in accountancy, and Jennifer, born in 1979, is reading English at Plymouth University with aspirations in the direction of publishing.

So in a sense, the wheel has come full circle: Michael's new-found leisure time has given him the opportunity to explore his family history. His first supervisor at Kingston Telephone Exchange was an Eric Pooley (quite possibly a relative and one of Edward's many descendants) and his researches have taken him back to 22 The Green, Richmond, a property belonging to the pension fund of which he is a beneficiary and where a century and a half ago the great-great-great grandfather of his daughters was running a school and in the process of raising a son who was to become one of the most famous and notorious cricketers of his generation.

LIST OF ILLUSTRATIONS

(between pages 96 and 97)

BIBLIOGRAPHY

BOOKS etc

Alverstone, Rt Hon Lord and Alcock, C W *Surrey Cricket: Its History and Associations*, Longman 1902

Bettesworth, W A *Chats on the Cricket Field* Merritt & Hatcher 1910

The Walkers of Southgate Methuen 1900

Birley, Sir Derek *A Social History of English Cricket* Aurum Press 1999

Caffyn, William *71 not out* Blackwood 1899

Daft, Richard *Kings of Cricket: Anecdotes and Reminiscences 1858 to 1892* Arrowsmith 1893

Digby, Anne *British Welfare Policy: Workhouse to Workfare* Faber and Faber 1989

Ford, W J *Middlesex County Cricket Club 1864-99*. Longman Green and Co 1900

Gardiner, Juliet & Wenborn, Neil (Ed) *The History Today Companion to British History* Collins & Brown 1995

Grace, W G *Cricket* Arrowsmith 1891

Harris, Lord (Ed) *The History of Kent County Cricket* Eyre and Spottiswoode 1907

Lord Hawke, Lord Harris and Sir Home Gordon *The Memorial Biography of W G Grace* Constable and Company Ltd 1919

Hutchinson, Horace G *Country Life Library of Sports - Cricket* George Newnes Ltd 1893

Jacks, Alasdair (Ed) *Chepstow Cricket Club: The First 150 Years* Chepstow C C 1988

Lascelles and Co *Gazetteer of the Counties of Monmouth and Hereford* 1852

Lemmon, David *Surrey County Cricket Club* Christopher Helm 1989

Frederick Lillywhite's Guide to Cricketers, 1862-66

*John (later John and James, then James) Lillywhite's Cricketers' Companion,*1865-84

James Lillywhite's Cricketers' Annual, 1872-84

Low, Robert *W G* Richard Cohen Books 1997

Midwinter, Eric (Ed) *Surrey County Cricket Club: 150 Years: A Celebration* Surrey Youth Cricket Ltd 1995

Darling Old Oval Cricket Lore Ltd 1995

Nissel, Muriel *People Count: A History of the General Register Office* HMSO 1987

Packham, Roger *The Troubles of Edward Pooley* Wisden Cricket Monthly October 1982

Pentelow, J N *England v Australia 1877 to 1904* Arrowsmith 1904

Pullin A W *Talks with Old English Cricketers* Blackwood 1900

Pycroft, James *Cricketana* Longman's 1865

The Cricket Field (edited by F S Ashley-Cooper) St James' Press, 1922

Rae, Simon *W G Grace: A Life* Faber and Faber 1998

Reese, T W *New Zealand Cricket 1841-1914* Simpson and Williams Ltd Christchurch 1927

Ross, Gordon *The Surrey Story* Stanley Paul 1957

Rundell, Michael *The Dictionary of Cricket* Guild Publishing 1988

Scorebooks 1861/83 Association of Cricket Statisticians and Historians

Scores and Biographies of Famous Cricketers Vols VII - XIV 1861-78

Sievwright, William *History of Perth Cricket Club 1826-81* [unpublished]

Sissons, Ric *The Players* Kingswood Press 1988

Steel, A G & Lyttelton, R H *Badminton Library of Sports and Pastimes* Longman, Green & Co 1889

The Stranger's Illustrated Guide to Chepstow and Its Neighbourhood Newman 1843

Surrey 1845-1945 Centenary (various authors)

Warner, Sir Pelham *Gentlemen v Players 1806-1949*   Harrap 1950

Waters, Ivor *The Town of Chepstow: Part 3: The Lower Town* The Chepstow Society
1973

Webber, J R *The Chronicle of W G*   Association of Cricket Statisticians and Historians
1998

Weinreb, Ben and Hibbert, Christopher *The London Encyclopædia* MacMillan 1983

West, G Derek *The Elevens of England* Darf Publishers 1988

    Twelve Days of Grace   Darf Publishers 1989

Wisden Cricketers' Almanack 1864-1908

NEWSPAPERS AND PERIODICALS

Belfast Newsletter
Bell's Life in London
Chepstow Weekly Advertiser
Cricket, A Weekly Record of the Game
Daily Telegraph
Keighley Herald
Licensing World
Monmouthshire Merlin
New Zealand Herald and Daily Southern Cross
Otago Daily Times
Otago Witness
Richmond and Twickenham Times
The Sporting Life
The Sportsman
Sunday Telegraph
Surrey Comet
The Times